Praise for Mary Rowland's
Best Practices for Financial Advisors

"This is the **best effort yet to put down ... the wisdom that has been gathering in the best financial planning practices around the country.** If you want to know **what some of the most thoughtful practitioners in the profession think** about practice management, ethics, marketing focus, regulation, compliance, and client relationships, **this is the best thing we have in print.**"

ROBERT N. VERES
Publisher, *Inside Information*

"If you are considering whether to add this book to your professional library, our advice would be similarly succinct. **'Just buy it'.**"

Journal of Financial Planning

"Do you want to succeed as a personal financial advisor? Get ten eminent practitioners to be your mentors. If you don't know ten, buy Mary Rowland's new book, *Best Practices for Financial Advisors.* She gleans hundreds of practical ideas from fifty-five successful professionals of every imaginable style, and presents them in her usual engaging prose. **You will find yourself underlining on almost every page. When you're finished, you'll be energized and probably want to read it again.**"

NAPFA Advisor

"Mary Rowland has more than 20 years covering this industry and all aspects of business and personal finance, including her column at the *New York Times* .... **Rowland identified fifty-five at the top of the profession for aspirants to chart their course by ....** The ethical superstars talk candidly about fees vs. commissions, state-by-state regulation issues, and all the baggage ... that comes along with professing to be a financial planner."

BookPage

"**[A] useful and thought provoking book** for anyone working as or considering a career as a planner. But even if you don't count yourself in that category, this book could be useful if you hire or plan to hire a planner .... **Rowland provides an insider's perspective** and describes practices that should set the standard for judging your own planner."

San Jose Mercury News

"She explains where to get the best training, which groups and conferences are valuable for networking, how to handle the press, how to market the services, and how best to charge for services .... The average reader ... can **learn not only what to look for in hiring an adviser but how to be a better client.**"

Library Journal

"This book is without doubt **the best description of what financial planners really do and the value they add.** It clearly describes the distinction between the 'feeling' skills ('virtually every planner ... had a connection to teaching') and the critical thinking skills required to be a top planner .... **Thanks to Mary Rowland for a book that so clearly helps me understand what I do for my clients now and what I may be doing for them in the future.**"

ROBERT V. HOROWITZ, CFA
New England Investment Management

"*Best Practices for Financial Advisors* is a great book. It is not only **the perfect orientation manual** for new employees to the field ... but a **wonderful learning tool** for the experienced advisor. We are ordering extra copies for everyone in the office."

RONALD W. ROGÉ, MS, CFP
Financial Advisory & Investment
Management Services

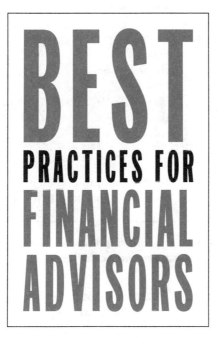

BEST
PRACTICES FOR
FINANCIAL
ADVISORS

Also available from
Bloomberg Press

The Financial Planner's Guide to
Moving Your Practice Online
by Douglas H. Durrie

Deena Katz on Practice Management:
for Financial Advisers, Planners, and Wealth Managers
by Deena B. Katz

Deena Katz's Tools and Templates for Your Practice:
for Financial Advisers, Planners, and Wealth Managers
by Deena B. Katz

Protecting Your Practice
by Katherine Vessenes, in cooperation with the
International Association for Financial Planning

A complete list of our titles is available at
www.bloomberg.com/books

Attention Corporations

BLOOMBERG PRESS BOOKS are available at quantity
discounts with bulk purchase for sales promotional
use and for corporate education or other business
uses. Special editions or book excerpts can also be
created. For information, please call 609-279-4670
or write to: Special Sales Dept., Bloomberg Press,
P.O. Box 888, Princeton, NJ 08542.

BLOOMBERG® WEALTH MANAGER magazine is the premiere
professional information resource for independent financial planners
and investment advisers who are serving clients of high net worth.
See wealth.bloomberg.com or call 1-800-681-7727.

BLOOMBERG PROFESSIONAL LIBRARY

MARY ROWLAND

BEST
PRACTICES FOR
FINANCIAL
ADVISORS

FOREWORD BY MICHAEL R. BLOOMBERG

Bloomberg Press
◆
PRINCETON

Books are available for bulk purchases at special discounts. For information, please write: Special Markets Department, Bloomberg Press.

BLOOMBERG, THE BLOOMBERG, BLOOMBERG BUSINESS NEWS, BLOOMBERG FINANCIAL MARKETS, BLOOMBERG PRESS, BLOOMBERG PROFESSIONAL LIBRARY, and BLOOMBERG PERSONAL BOOKSHELF are trademarks and service marks of Bloomberg L.P. All rights reserved.

This publication is designed to provide accurate and authoritative information. It is sold with the understanding that the publisher is not engaged in rendering legal, accounting, investment-planning, or other professional services. If legal advice or other expert assistance is required, the services of a competent professional person should be sought.

First edition published 1997, updated imprint 2002.

3 5 7 9 10 8 6 4 2

Rowland, Mary.

    Best practices for financial advisors / Mary Rowland ; foreword by Michael R. Bloomberg.

       p.   cm. — (Bloomberg professional library)

    Includes bibliographical references and index.

    ISBN 1-57660-006-8 (alk. paper)

    1. Financial planners—United States. 2. Investment advisors—United States. 3. Investments—United States.   I. Title.

II. Series.

HG181.R67 1997   96-52818

332.6' 068—dc21   CIP

Acquired and edited by Christine Miles

Book design by Don Morris Design

For Chris Miles,
my favorite editor

CONTENTS

FOREWORD

BY MICHAEL R. BLOOMBERG

MARY ROWLAND FOUND that some remark-

ably high standards have been set for the

planning profession—not by regulators,

consumer groups, or trade associations, but

by the practices of the best financial advi-

sors. How do these industry leaders exceed

their clients' expectations? How do they

stay current, prioritize, structure their fees,

cope with competition, anticipate change, come up with profitable ideas?

And how can you apply their knowledge to grow your business? What strategies should you be using? What shortcuts must you avoid? What about disclosure, suitability, legal liability, and audits? How can you tell a sleeping dog from a ticking bomb?

IN THIS BOOK YOU'LL HEAR from experts. See what Harold Evensky, Cynthia Meyers, Bob Willard, Bert Whitehead, and others have to say about which fee schedules work best. Dip into Chapter 6, "What's Right for a Client?" for Ross Levin's ideas on suitability, and what he tells a client who calls about private placements. Or turn to Chapter 4, "Accepting a Fiduciary Role," for Andy Hudick's thoughts on registering and setting up documentation, and Jack Blankinship's and James Wilson's suggestions on fiduciary requirements.

A Few Notes on the Format

◆ This book puts a lot of information into a small package. It is designed to be functional as well as factual, trim enough to be carried in a coat pocket and taken on the road, read easily on train, ship, or plane.
◆ The book's organization takes your hectic schedule into account. The material flows logically and offers at every turn real-world applications.
◆ Our graphics are designed with the busy reader in mind, highlighting important concepts from the experts in color every couple of pages.

BY SOME ESTIMATES, there are 300,000 people in the U.S. offering services as financial advisors. That concerns anyone who has worked hard to get to the top of the profession, build a reputation, master the details, and develop a client base.

Consumer demand for financial guidance, driven by the popularity (and necessity) of self-directed retirement vehicles—such as IRAs, 401(k)s, and 403(b)s— is pulling hundreds of new practitioners into the field every week. These players range from sole proprietors and small financial-management shops to energetic new arms at large blue-chip brokerage houses and mutual-fund companies.

Among this orderly stampede into the storefront are inevitably some arrivals nearly as perplexed as, and not much better-qualified than, the clients they aim to advise. This reminds many veterans and some older investors of how the field's quality control sagged in the 1980s, during the heyday of tax-advantaged limited partnerships, looser restrictions on IRAs, and ebullient stock market share prices.

The most experienced and successful planners, like the ones you hear from in this book, want to see high standards created and maintained by the planning community itself. A reputation for strong ethics, efficiency, and reliability is good for any profession. More concretely, regulators will move into a vacuum of accountability. Witness the step-up in enforcement efforts by the National Association of Securities Dealers, and moves by the SEC to broaden the makeup of the Financial Accounting Standards Board.

I believe Mary Rowland and the top advisors who cooperated on this project deliver valuable perspective—true business intelligence—on what works in the marketplace. These are things you can use today to be ready for the day after tomorrow. I think you will find the book a trustworthy tool for making your practice the best it can be.

INTRODUCTION

BEST PRACTICES FOR FINANCIAL ADVISORS

IN THE 20-ODD YEARS THAT I have worked

as a business and personal finance re-

porter—half a dozen of them as a colum-

nist for *The New York Times*—I have written

scores of stories about unscrupulous finan-

cial advisors of all stripes. One *Times* col-

umn looked at a California insurance agent

who sent a letter to 30,000 teachers warning them that they had purchased insurance from a disreputable company. His letter read, in part: "The United States District Court has determined that it is in your best interest to review and consider a choice of carriers as an alternative to your current policy."

Pretty scary. Actually, the reason he was so familiar with these policies was that he'd sold them in the first place. But now he'd had a feud with his old insurance company. He'd switched to a new one, and he wanted the teachers to drop their old contracts—even though it meant paying a substantial penalty—and move with him. (Insurance agents will recognize this as "twisting," a practice that is illegal in many states.) He and the original insurer were locked in a court battle, and he used that court case to throw a scare into the teachers. The court did *not*, of course, recommend that the teachers consider dropping their policies. In fact, the court ordered *him* to drop the issue.

Another story followed two elderly women who took their lump-sum retirement money to their local bank in Connecticut, where they were sold a "guaranteed" investment. It turned out to be a global currency fund, which immediately began hemorrhaging.

Another piece explored an investment called "The Money Tree," which was sold to a retired executive for his grandson as a college-savings vehicle promising "maximum safety, high yields, tax-deferred growth, and tax-free income." It turned out to be a life-insurance policy. He didn't find that out until he received the annual premium statement the following year.

What common problem do we have here? Unsuitable investments? Lack of disclosure?

Inadequate due diligence? Failure to register as an investment advisor? No. The common theme is greed. There are plenty of charlatans in the financial services industry who prey on the unsuspecting in different ways. But they are linked by greed and incompetence.

So when I was asked to write a compliance guide for financial advisors, I was intrigued. Yet I suspected that the greedy and incompetent aren't really interested in compliance. They won't rush out to buy a guide that will teach them how to do a better job. Worse yet, many of the practices that reasonable people might consider question-able—if not deceptive—are not precisely illegal. Financial planning is a rapidly grow-ing business. But it has few rules and regu-lations. In fact, anyone can call himself a financial planner, advisor, or consultant with no training or credentials whatsoever. And he can charge whatever he likes to do it.

There are, of course, some regulations for advisors who fall within certain niches of the profession. For example, those who pro-vide investment advice and manage more than $25 million in assets must register as investment advisors with the Securities and

Exchange Commission under the Investment Advisers Act of 1940. Advisors who manage less than $25 million are regulated by the states, as of April 1997. Those who sell securities or mutual funds must carry a Series 6 or a Series 7 securities license. And those who sell insurance products must be licensed by each of the states in which they do business. (Insurance agents who sell products with a mutual-fund wrapper must have a Series 6 license as well.)

I dutifully ordered all the legal books containing these regulations and waded through them. The problem, still, was that there were too many loopholes.

So I decided to turn the problem around and look at it from the other side. Even though the profession is unregulated—or perhaps *because* it is unregulated—an elite cadre of advisors has emerged from the mass of 300,000 or so financial advisors and consultants, and they are dead serious about elevating the status of their profession. They are Harvard MBAs, engineers from MIT, former teachers, social workers, stockbrokers, accountants, and other committed professionals who are striving to change the face of financial planning.

These men and women are not interested in merely achieving the minimal necessary compliance as advisors. Their goal is to continually raise the bar. How to do that? They read a lot. They attend the requisite conferences, retreats, and meetings. They form networking and study groups to learn from one another. And they are always on the prowl for better information about asset classes, better ways to understand and educate clients, new measurements of risk and return, improved software, private letter rulings that influence retirement distributions or pension plans—anything that will affect the financial health of their clients. Many of them specialize in specific areas of planning involving investments, corporate executives, retirement, family business, divorce, or women's issues. Others do broad comprehensive financial planning.

This guide focuses on what these planners are doing. Few of their business practices are actual requirements for operating as a financial planner. Instead they reflect the thinking at the top of the profession—the best practices for financial advisors.

To start, I identified 55 financial advisors who are considered by their peers—and by journalists and others in the field—to be among the best in the business. The list is by no means exhaustive. Inevitably, there were some fine planners who fell beneath my radar screen. That's why we're not calling them the 55 *best* planners in America. But the planners on the list are at the top of their field. Many of them are sources I have used for years. I kept going back to them because of their knowledge, their integrity, and their dedication to their profession. Most are now or have been leaders of industry trade and professional groups. Nearly all of them are well known as speakers in their specialities. They come from all over the country.

These planners agreed to participate in interviews and conference calls on the workings of their business. One of the most fascinating things about the calls was the diversity of people operating in the same profession. One call combined Sharon Rich, a planner in Belmont, Massachusetts, who works by herself in a home office doing pure fee-by-the-hour planning, and Carol Caruthers, who is chief executive officer of a family office in St. Paul where she has 60 employees, including vice presidents in charge of investments and trusts. One of the commonalities linking Rich and Caruthers—and the other participants—is pursuit of excellence in planning. I think the result is an interesting and unusual compilation of how some of the best minds in the business are striving to better serve their clients and peers. I hope it sets you to thinking, too.

THE PLANNERS

HERE ARE THE PLANNERS who participated in our best-practices guide:

GINGER APPLEGARTH, from Winchester, Massachusetts, is a fee-only financial planner with a specialty in insurance and investment planning. Applegarth, who appears regularly on CNBC's "The Money Club" and on the "Today" show, has also appeared on "The Oprah Winfrey Show." Her book, "The Money Diet: Reaping the Rewards of Financial Fitness," appeared on several best-seller lists and is available on audiocassette. An honors graduate of Vanderbilt University, Applegarth was the youngest person to earn the certified financial planner designation.

   10 Mount Vernon St.
   Winchester, MA 01890
   617-721-5445
   Fax: 617-721-0385

MARK BALASA, a certified public accountant, specializes in investment management from Schaumburg,

Illinois. He is past president of the Chicago chapter of the International Association for Financial Planning.

Burton Investment Management, Inc.

921 N. Plum Grove Rd.

Schaumburg, IL 60173

847-517-4300

Fax: 847-517-4312

ELAINE E. BEDEL was director of personal financial planning at Coopers & Lybrand and a trust officer at Indiana National Bank before becoming a fee-only financial planner. Bedel took a break from planning in 1994 and 1995 to serve as director of the Department of Metropolitan Development for the city of Indianapolis.

9190 Priority Way West Dr., Suite 120

Indianapolis, IN 46240

317-843-1358

Fax: 317-574-5999

JOHN T. BLANKINSHIP JR. is one of the best-known planners in a business in which he has worked for nearly 30 years. Blankinship, who does comprehensive planning from Del Mar, California, has served as president and chairman of the Institute of Certified Financial Planners, as well as a member of the board of governors for the CFP Board of Standards, Inc.

2775 Via De La Valle, Suite 201

Del Mar, CA 92014

619-755-5166

Fax: 619-755-5358

ELEANOR K. H. BLAYNEY is director of portfolio management for Sullivan, Bruyette, Speros & Blayney Inc., a financial planning firm in McLean, Virginia. She majored in English and French at Mount Holyoke College and Cambridge University, United Kingdom, and received an MBA from the University of Chicago, where she specialized in finance and international business. She is perhaps best known in the business for her thoughtful presentations on investing and measuring risk.

8180 Greensboro Dr., Suite 450
McLean, VA 22102
703-734-9330
Fax: 703-356-2549

NORMAN M. BOONE, a Harvard MBA, was a banker, a chief financial officer, a college teacher, and a U.S. Army officer before he became a financial planner in 1987. Boone is particularly interested in using the computer and the Internet in his planning practice and has given a number of presentations on tech-savvy planning. He concentrates on planning for family business.

1 Post St., Suite 2750
San Francisco, CA 94104
415-788-1952
Fax: 415-788-7105

GARY N. BOWYER, a fee-only planner in Chicago, serves on the board of the National Association of Personal Financial Advisors (NAPFA). Bowyer earned a bachelor's degree from Purdue and an MBA in finance from Boston University. He held management and marketing positions with Control Data Corp., ITT, and Mellon Bank before becoming a planner specializing in retirement planning and planning for business owners.

6405 N. Avondale
Chicago, IL 60631
773-631-8070
Fax: 773-631-0981

STANLEY H. BREITBARD created the personal financial planning specialty at Price Waterhouse, building a national practice with 15 offices and registering a Price Waterhouse affiliate with the Securities and Exchange Commission as an investment advisor. He also served as the first chairman of the executive committee for the personal financial planning division of the American Institute of Certified Public Accountants (AICPA).

751 Holmby Ave.
Los Angeles, CA 90024
310-474-4845
Fax: 310-474-4003

JAMES L. BUDROS has worked in the financial planning and trust industries for more than 25 years. He was the first chairperson of the CFP Board of Standards, Inc. and serves on the CFP board of governors. Budros reviews restaurants for Ohio public radio in his weekly program "Table Hopping" and has won numerous cooking awards and appeared on many television cooking shows, including one where he prepared an original lobster and scallop recipe with Craig Claiborne, who was then food editor of *The New York Times.*

1650 Lake Shore Dr., Suite 150
Columbus, OH 43204
614-481-6900
Fax: 614-481-6919

DAVID H. BUGEN, who earned an MBA in finance from Rutgers University, is former chairman of the Northern New Jersey chapter of the International Association for Financial Planning. He does comprehensive financial planning from Morristown, New Jersey.

Individual Asset Planning Corp.
65 Madison Ave.
Morristown, NJ 07960
201-539-2300
Fax: 201-539-1713

MARILYN R. CAPELLI DIMITROFF, a financial planner for 20 years, is a former senior vice president and private banking manager at Citizens Bank in Michigan and Illinois, where she established and managed a financial advisory and private banking division. She focuses on planning for professionals and business owners.

Capelli Financial Services
2050 N. Woodward Ave., Suite 140
Bloomfield Hills, MI 48304

810-594-9282

Fax: 810-594-5751

CAROL R. CARUTHERS is president and chief executive officer of Fiduciary Counselling Inc., which oversees trusts, estates, and foundations, and provides financial services to clients of privately held corporations and partnerships. She was previously national partner in charge of personal financial services at Price Waterhouse.

332 Minnesota St., Suite 2100

St. Paul, MN 55101

612-215-4404

Fax: 612-215-4486

MICHAEL J. CHASNOFF, a fee-only planner in Cincinnati, does comprehensive planning, concentrating in retirement and insurance planning.

9477 Kenwood Rd.

Cincinnati, OH 45242

513-792-6648

Fax: 513-792-6645

DAVID H. DIESSLIN, who earned an MBA from the University of Dallas, founded his Fort Worth–based financial planning firm in 1980. He is former president and chairman of the National Association of Personal Financial Advisors. He has also served as chairman of the Fort Worth Business and Estate Council and as a board member of the Fort Worth Opera. He focuses on planning for business owners.

303 Main St., Suite 200

Fort Worth, TX 76102

817-332-6122

Fax: 817-335-4839

ROY T. DILIBERTO has 30 years' experience in the financial planning industry, where he started in life insurance and then moved to comprehensive planning. Diliberto recently set up a client advisory board to seek input from clients on what kind of reports they want and how best to serve their needs.

RTD Financial Advisors Inc.
2 Penn Center
Philadelphia, PA 19102
215-557-3800
Fax: 215-557-3814

DAVID J. DRUCKER, who received his MBA from American University in Washington, was a financial analyst in the government and a director of finance in private industry before becoming a financial planner in 1981. He concentrates in planning for retirement-age couples, widows, and professionals.

Malgoire Drucker Inc.
4720 Montgomery Lane, Suite 210
Bethesda, MD 20814
301-656-3999
Fax: 301-656-0935

HAROLD R. EVENSKY, who earned his bachelor's and master's degrees in engineering, business, and finance from Cornell University, is arguably the best-known financial planner in the area of investment management. He is well loved by the media for his willingness to offer blunt, pithy statements that make great quotes on a wide range of financial planning topics. Evensky is a member of the CFP board of governors, chair of the board of appeals, and president of the Florida Gold Coast Chapter of the American Association of Individual Investors. He is the author of "Wealth Management."

241 Sevilla Ave., Suite 902
Coral Gables, FL 33134
305-448-8882
Fax: 305-448-1326

CHARLES D. HAINES JR., who has an MBA from the University of Virginia, set up his fee-only financial planning firm in 1986. Because Haines sees training financial planners as one of the biggest challenges for the industry in the next decade, he sponsors a scholarship in financial planning at the University of Alabama.

1 Independence Plaza, Suite 614
Birmingham, AL 35209
205-871-3334
Fax: 205-879-1114

STANLEY E. HARGRAVE, a principal at Hall & Vernazza, a CPA firm in Riverside, California, specializes in personal financial planning and investment management services. Much of his work involves representing financial planners and stockbrokers in disputes involving due diligence.

3714 Tibbets St., Suite 100
Riverside, CA 92506
909-781-7320
Fax: 909-682-1382

DAVID E. HOMRICH graduated magna cum laude from the University of Georgia, received a master's degree in accountancy, and began his career with Price Waterhouse, the Big Six accounting firm, before setting up a financial planning firm in 1989. He is coauthor, with Harold W. Gourgues, of "Total Financial Planning: A Guide for Financial Advisors and Serious Investors."

1 Buckhead Plaza, Suite 830
3060 Peachtree Rd. NW
Atlanta, GA 30305
404-264-1400
Fax: 404-237-5114

H. LYNN HOPEWELL, who earned an MBA from Harvard Business School, has been a financial planner since 1980. He is credited by his peers with vastly improving the *Journal of Financial Planning* when he served as editor of that magazine. Hopewell served as the technical advisor to Intuit for the development of the Quicken Financial Planner software. He is a member of the board of governors of the CFP Board of Standards, Inc.

The Monitor Group
12450 Fair Lakes Circle, Suite 650

Fairfax, VA 22033
703-968-3002
Fax: 703-968-3005

WILLIAM B. HOWARD JR. specializes in financial planning for physicians. He served on the CFP Board of Standards, Inc. and is chair of the Mid-South Society of the Institute of Certified Financial Planners.

6410 Poplar Ave., Suite 330
Memphis, TN 38119
901-761-5068
Fax: 901-761-2217

ANDREW M. HUDICK is a graduate of the University of Virginia's school of engineering. A fee-only financial planner since 1981, Hudick has been a member of the CFP Board of Standards, Inc. since its inception. He was president of the National Association of Personal Financial Advisors (NAPFA) for 1995–96, and focuses on planning for business owners.

P. O. Box 12386
Roanoke, VA 24025
540-342-7102

DEENA B. KATZ is president of Evensky, Brown, Katz & Levitt, a Coral Gables, Florida, financial planning firm. Katz, who has a specialty in long-term care, speaks widely on that topic and is coauthor of "Planning for Long Term Health Care."

241 Sevilla Ave., Suite 902
Coral Gables, FL 33134
305-448-8882
Fax: 305-448-1326

STUART KESSLER is a senior tax partner at Goldstein, Golub, Kessler & Co. in New York. In October 1997, he will become chairman of the American Institute of Certified Public Accountants (AICPA). He is past president of the New York State Society of CPAs and has served on the board of the New York Estate Planning Council. He specializes in planning for executives and business owners.

1185 Ave. of Americas
New York, NY 10036
212-372-1304
Fax: 212-372-8304

GEORGE D. KINDER, a Harvard graduate, maintains a financial planning practice in Cambridge, where he spends six months of the year, and one in Maui, where he spends the other six. Kinder believes that life is too short to spend all of it saving for retirement. He encourages clients to pursue their other dreams as well, and he puts his money where his mouth is.

4 Brattle St.
Cambridge, MA 02138
617-864-6065
Fax: 617-576-5180

JANE V. KING, who has 25 years' experience in the investment business, including executive positions at two mutual fund groups, set up her own firm a dozen years ago. She is on the board of the Women's Economic Roundtable. King's specialities include working with women, nontraditional partners, and business owners, as well as handling investment and estate planning, severance packages, and buyout offers.

Fairfield Financial Advisors, Ltd.
20 William St.
Wellesley, MA 02181
617-431-1119
Fax: 617-431-7611

S. TIMOTHY KOCHIS specializes in comprehensive financial planning for corporate executives and professionals at Kochis Fitz Tracy & Gorman in San Francisco. He was formerly national director of personal financial planning for Deloitte & Touche and for the Bank of America Executive Financial Counseling Group. Kochis, who has also earned a master's degree in business administration and a law degree, has been president of the CFP Board of Standards, Inc. and chairman of its board of examiners.

450 Sansome St., Suite 1600
San Francisco, CA 94111
415-394-6668, ext. 68
Fax: 415-394-6676

RAM KOLLURI earned a bachelor's degree in mathematics and an MBA in finance. Kolluri specializes in money management.

Individual Asset Planning Corp.
103 Carnegie Center, Suite 100
Princeton, NJ 08540
609-452-2929
Fax: 609-452-0048

DIAHANN W. LASSUS served in management positions at a number of corporations, including Xerox and AT&T, before setting up a financial planning firm in New Providence, New Jersey, where she offers fee-only financial planning, money management, accounting, management advisory services, and tax preparation. She serves on the board of governors of the CFP Board of Standards, Inc. and chairs the certification committee.

1 Academy St.
New Providence, NJ 07974
908-464-0102
Fax: 908-464-9852

ROSS LEVIN, past chairman of the International Association for Financial Planning, is author of "Wealth Management Index." He specializes in investment management and portfolio planning.

Accredited Investors Inc.
Lake Calhoun Executive Center
3033 Excelsior Blvd., Suite 185
Minneapolis, MN 55416
612-725-6820
Fax: 612-928-0349

LINDA S. LUBITZ does comprehensive financial planning with specialties in planning during divorce and planning for widows, from Miami. She served as chairperson for the 1996 Conference for Advanced Planning in Phoenix. Lubitz is also coauthor of "The Investment Policy Guidebook." Her most challenging client to date has been a postal worker who won $24 million in the Florida lottery. Working with him has taught Lubitz a lot, she says, "about what money can and cannot buy."

9130 S. Dadeland Blvd., Suite 1600
Miami, FL 33156
305-670-0545
Fax: 305-670-0636

MARY A. MALGOIRE, who has an MBA degree from the University of Santa Clara, is past president and chairman of the board of the National Association of Personal Financial Advisors (NAPFA). She has testified before both the U.S. Congress and the Maryland state legislature on proposed legislation for financial planners.

Malgoire Drucker Inc.
4720 Montgomery Lane, Suite 210
Bethesda, MD 20814
301-656-3999
Fax: 301-656-0935

KATHARINE A. McGEE does fee-only comprehensive financial planning from St. Louis. A member of the National Association of Personal Financial Advisors, she served on the NAPFA board in 1995.

8112 Stratford Dr.
St. Louis, MO 63105
314-863-1867
Fax: 314-863-1868

MARY P. MERRILL specializes in comprehensive financial planning for doctors, executives, and small-business owners from Madison, Wisconsin. Merrill has a BA from Cornell University and an MBA from the University of Wisconsin. For four years, she headed the financial planning department at First Wisconsin National Bank in Madison.

150 E. Gilman St., Suite 150
Madison, WI 53703
608-255-5469
Fax: 608-255-5043

CYNTHIA S. MEYERS believes that "a successful life, like a successful business, is guided by a mission or purpose." She identifies that mission in her own life and helps clients to do the same thing. Meyers, who was an editor of children's books before she earned her MBA and became a financial planner in 1982, acts in local theater, sings in her church choir, and rollerblades.

455 University Ave., Suite 201
Sacramento, CA 95825
916-927-6487
Fax: 916-922-0827

KYRA HOLLOWELL MORRIS specializes in taxes, small businesses, asset management, and estate planning from Charleston, South Carolina. Morris, who has a degree in electrical engineering and takes karate lessons, heads the society relations committee for the Institute of Certified Financial Planners. At the ICFP Retreat in Traverse City, Michigan, she could be found attending seminars in the morning, leading the troops up the sand dunes around Lake Michigan in the afternoon, and organizing a dance in the evening.

Morris Financial Concepts
107 Pitt St.
Mt. Pleasant, SC 29464
803-884-6192
Fax: 803-884-6937

GARY PITTSFORD specializes in portfolio management and financial planning for small-business owners. Pittsford was founding president of NAPFA and has served as a member of the board and of the ethics committee for the International Association for Financial Planning.

8335 Allison Point Trail, Suite 190
Indianapolis, IN 46250

317-849-9559

Fax: 317-577-8575

BARBARA J. POPE, a certified public accountant, was the partner in charge of the personal financial services practice for Price Waterhouse in Chicago. She is now the chief executive of a family office.

115 S. LaSalle St.

Chicago, IL 60603

312-853-6630

Fax: 312-853-1860

SHARON RICH, who earned a doctorate in education from Harvard University with a focus on women's psychological development, operates a fee-only financial planning practice that focuses on money and relationships, divorce, nontraditional families, debt management, inherited wealth, and socially responsible investing.

76 Townsend Rd.

Belmont, MA 02178

617-489-3601

Fax: 617-489-2666

RONALD W. ROGÉ does comprehensive financial planning from Long Island, New York. As chairman of the public relations committee for the National Association of Personal Financial Advisors, he is largely responsible for the glowing press coverage NAPFA has received throughout the 1990s.

2100 Middle Country Rd.

Centereach, NY 11720

516-471-2786

Fax: 516-471-2917

PEGGY RUHLIN gave financial commentary on a weekly program on National Public Radio for two years. Trained as a certified public accountant and then as a financial planner, she is former president of the International Association for Financial Planning.

1650 Lake Shore Dr., Suite 150

Columbus, OH 43204

614-481-6900
Fax: 614-481-6919

MYRA SALZER, a fee-only planner in Boulder, Colorado, specializes in financial planning for inheritors. Salzer, who started her career as a chemical engineer, set up her fee-only planning firm in 1983. She conducts workshops that focus on the problems of inherited wealth.

1919 14th St., Suite 319
Boulder, CO 80302
303-444-1919
Fax: 303-444-1479

JUDITH A. SHINE, who specializes in retirement planning, will complete her master of science degree in financial planning in 1997. She chairs the editorial advisory board of the *Journal of Financial Planning* and is a member of the Charles Schwab advisory board.

Shine Investment Advisory Services Inc.
6143 S. Willow Dr., Suite 100
Englewood, CO 80111
303-740-8600
Fax: 303-290-0237

LOUIS P. STANASOLOVICH served on the board of the International Association for Financial Planning, as well as on a number of committees, including the ethics committee. As a member of that group's investment committee, he managed a third of its endowment money.

105 Braunlich Dr., Suite 250
Pittsburgh, PA 15237
412-635-9210
Fax: 412-635-9213

GREGORY D. SULLIVAN earned his accounting degree from Pennsylvania State University in 1979 and worked for an international accounting firm before becoming a financial planner in 1985. In 1996, he served as chairman of the International Association for Financial Planning and has been a member of the board since 1989.

8180 Greensboro Dr., Suite 450
McLean, VA 22102
703-734-9300
Fax: 703-356-2549

LAURA TARBOX, who specializes in retirement planning, investments, and employee benefits, teaches
financial planning at the University of Southern California, where she started a financial planning intern-
ship program and does curriculum development and
career counseling.

500 Newport Center Dr., Suite 500
Newport Beach, CA 92660
714-721-2330
Fax: 714-721-0734

JOHN W. UELEKE, who has a background in mathematics, physics, and finance, is a financial planner in
Memphis.

Middle South Advisory Corp.
1755 Kirby Parkway, Suite 330
Memphis, TN 38120
901-758 9006
Fax: 901-758-9007

ROBERT E. WACKER, a comprehensive financial
planner specializing in retirement planning and services for professionals, in San Luis Obispo, California,
is past president and chairman of the board of the
National Association of Personal Financial Advisors
(NAPFA). He sits on the board of governors and is
chairman of the board of appeals of the CFP Board of
Standards., Inc.

1159 Marsh St.
San Luis Obispo, CA 93401
805-541-1308
Fax: 805-541-5517

STEVEN B. WEINSTEIN is a partner in Andersen
Worldwide and managing director of Arthur Andersen Financial Advisers, the registered investment advi-

sor that oversees investment advisors. He has a law degree from Northwestern University and holds the chartered financial analyst (CFA) designation. Weinstein also serves on the board of governors of the CFP Board of Standards, Inc. and on the CCH Financial and Estate Planning Advisory Board.

Arthur Andersen LLP
33 W. Monroe St., 03-24
Chicago, IL 60603
312-507-7206
Fax: 312-507-1009

BERT WHITEHEAD got his start in financial services in 1956, at the age of 12, when he was hired as a "board boy"—he scribbled current stock prices on the board—at E.F. Hutton in Bisbee, Arizona. Whitehead then earned a degree in psychology, an MBA, and a law degree before becoming a financial planner. He is founder of Cambridge Associates, a company that helps planners convert from commissions to fees.

Franklin Village Office Centre
26111 W. Fourteen Mile Road, Suite 100
Franklin, MI 48025
810-737-7090
Fax: 810-737-7094

ROBERT E. WILLARD traveled the world as a child while his father was a senior U.S. military officer, a career that Willard, too, set his sights on. When he decided he was too much a nonconformist, Willard turned to financial planning, where he helps clients such as physicians and business owners make direct investments in real estate and other types of businesses.

P.O. Box 7
Colorado Springs, CO 80901
719-473-2200
Fax: 719-473-2202

JAMES E. WILSON formed South Carolina's first fee-only financial planning and investment management firm in 1982. He is past president of the National Association of Personal Financial Advisors (NAPFA) and a former member of the board of governors of the CFP Board of Standards, Inc. Wilson, who served as a member of a blue-ribbon committee that reviewed South Carolina securities laws, specializes in planning for physicians and business owners.

P.O. Box 8393
Columbia, SC 29202
803-799-9203
Fax: 803-254-4474

ROBERT C. WINFIELD specializes in financial planning during divorce. He is a trained mediator who often serves as an expert witness, and he lectures to legal, financial, and mediation groups on planning for divorce.

Middle South Advisory Corp.
1755 Kirby Parkway, Suite 330
Memphis, TN 38120
901-758-9006
Fax: 901-758-9007

VIOLET P. WOODHOUSE, who worked as a financial planner specializing in divorce, decided in 1990 to return to law school to fill in her knowledge of matrimonial law. When she finished, she began to practice as a divorce lawyer, but continues to keep her financial planning credentials up to snuff to advise clients on property division.

2372 S.E. Bristol St., Suite A
Newport Beach, CA 92660
714-660-9215
Fax: 714-660-9216

ALPHABET

S O U P

TODAY, EVERYONE IN THE financial services

business seems to be a financial planner or

a financial consultant. But what's behind

these names? The financial planning pro-

fession is still largely unregulated. There is

no one set of initials that distinguish a plan-

ner as top-notch, the way an M.D. distin-

guishes a man or woman of medicine. But

there are several sets of letters bandied about in the business that are meaningful. Here are some of them:

CHARTERED FINANCIAL ANALYST (CFA) is a designation from the Association for Investment Management and Research in Charlottesville, Virginia (804-980-3668) to those who have completed a three-year program focusing on investment analysis. The program is considered rigorous and the designation a meaningful one, particularly for money managers and stock analysts.

CERTIFIED FINANCIAL PLANNER (CFP) has become the must-have designation for financial planners. It is issued by the CFP Board of Standards, Inc. in Denver (888-237-6275) to applicants who pass a ten-hour exam and agree to abide by a code of ethics. The CFP Board has been working hard for the past several years to upgrade the CFP designation to make it more like the certified public accountant designation. For example, the exam was rewritten and made much more difficult. In the spring of 1995, the board invited reporters to take the exam to see just how difficult it is to become a financial planner. (The exam was tough.) Although the CFP designation is now clearly the one to have, it does not follow, unfortunately, that everyone who has the designation is a top-notch planner. But if you're in the business, you need a CFP. If you're a consumer looking for a planner, you want a CFP. There were 32,000 planners with the CFP designation at the beginning of 1997.

THE CFP BOARD OF STANDARDS, INC. is the regulatory body for the 32,000 certified financial planners.

THE INSTITUTE OF CERTIFIED FINANCIAL PLANNERS (ICFP) is a national professional association with 11,000 CFP members.

THE COLLEGE FOR FINANCIAL PLANNING is one of the colleges that trains financial planners.

At one time, the above three groups—the CFP

Board, the Institute of Certified Financial Planners, and the College for Financial Planning—were under one roof. Today, they are three separate entities: one for regulation, one for networking and other professional functions, and one for education.

CERTIFIED PUBLIC ACCOUNTANT (CPA) is a designation regulated by the board of accountancy in each state. CPAs have a lot going for them. A CPA must pass a wide-ranging and rigorous test. Surveys show that CPAs are the most trusted and respected of financial service professionals. And Charlie Haines, a planner in Birmingham, Alabama, who has done considerable research on how to train financial planners for his business, believes that CPAs make the best candidates. Still, a CPA designation by itself does not mean that a person is a qualified financial planner. Those CPAs who are serious about financial planning—like David Homrich in Atlanta and Steve Weinstein in Chicago—get a CFP designation.

CHARTERED LIFE UNDERWRITER (CLU) is an insurance specialist trained by The American College in Bryn Mawr, Pennsylvania (610-526-1000). A CLU has three years of experience in the field of insurance, and has completed ten college-level insurance courses. Many fine people are CLUs—like Ben G. Baldwin, author of "The New Life Insurance Investment Advisor." But sporting a CLU does not make someone an expert in financial planning. It qualifies them to sell insurance. (Baldwin also has a CFP.) Many fine financial planners, like Roy Diliberto in Philadelphia and John Ueleke in Memphis, started as life insurance agents and moved into financial planning, getting their CFP in the process.

The American College also issues the designation of **CHARTERED FINANCIAL CONSULTANT (CHFC)** to those insurance agents who take three more courses. This, too, is an insurance designation. Expect someone who has a ChFC—but not a CFP—designation to

propose life insurance as a solution to your problem.
INTERNATIONAL ASSOCIATION FOR FINANCIAL PLANNING (IAFP) is a trade association based in Atlanta (800-945-4237) that is open to everyone in the financial services business. It has about 15,000 members. There are no specific requirements for membership, but members must sign a code of ethics. This group has made a comeback in the last few years as a source of training, education, and networking for financial planners.

NATIONAL ASSOCIATION OF PERSONAL FINANCIAL ADVISORS (NAPFA), based in Buffalo Grove, Illinois (708-537-7722), is a trade group of about 300 fee-only planners with strict admission requirements governing compensation. (There are an additional 200 associate members who are not strictly fee-only.) NAPFA members are not permitted to accept any commissions with the exception of trailing commissions on business that was transacted before they became a member.

NAPFA has created considerable controversy—and animosity—largely because some zealous members have suggested that NAPFA members alone are on the high road. Still, many planners who had avoided the organization for that reason, like Marilyn Capelli, have recently joined to take advantage of its excellent services. Capelli likes the educational seminars, she likes the referral systems (where she gets some of her best clients), and she likes the e-mail queries, which often teach her something about planning.

PERSONAL FINANCIAL SPECIALIST (PFS) is a credential given by the AICPA (American Institute of Certified Public Accountants, 800-862-4272) to members who have experience in personal finance and who pass an exam. It's a good idea, but it doesn't seem to have caught on like the CFP. Most CPAs have elected instead to get a CFP designation.

REGISTERED REPRESENTATIVE is a stockbroker

who has passed a series of securities exams and is registered with a broker/dealer and regulated by the National Association of Securities Dealers. Registered reps need not—and often do not—do financial planning. In fact, many financial planners argue that a registered rep is a securities salesman, versus a financial planner who looks at all of a client's needs.

REGISTERED INVESTMENT ADVISOR (RIA) is an individual or firm that has filed with the Securities and Exchange Commission. The RIA designation does not mean that the firm or individual is approved in any way by the SEC. In fact, the SEC will not allow RIAs to use the initials on their business cards because officials fear that it would imply some stamp of approval. But it does show that the advisor is in compliance with the registration requirement.

Under the National Securities Markets Improvement Act, which takes effect in April 1997, the SEC will regulate—and audit—RIAs with more than $25 million in assets under management. States will be responsible for advisors with less than $25 million in assets.

Experts caution advisors to expect overlapping regulation and to consider dual registration as this new system gets under way. For example, if your firm is managing $24.8 million in assets, you may not want to keep your SEC registration in 1997. Make a point to stay current as the new rules unfold.

EDUCATION & TRAINING

BEST PRACTICE Get your CFP designation.

Listen, learn all you can, and remember that

you are the teacher.

Let's start with three facts:

Fact Number 1: The meat of financial plan-

ning—investments, insurance, pensions,

estates, and trusts—is growing increasingly

complex, sprouting subspecialties in such

narrow niches as distributions from retire-

ment plans.

Fact Number 2: As baby boomers march

toward retirement, the largest generation

in history is searching for help with this

arcane stuff. And educated baby boomers

don't want help from a salesperson. They

want an objective advisor.

Put these two facts together and it's not surprising that Americans are flooding into financial planning. They include college grads looking for a growth career, middle-aged veterans of corporate downsizing, and early retirees, not to mention the thousands of brokers, bankers, and insurance agents who see the handwriting on the wall in their sales jobs. "Financial planning is certainly the place to be," says Robert Clark, editor in chief of the *Dow Jones Investment Advisor,* a publication for financial planners. "Virtually everyone in the financial services industry, whether they are brokers, bankers, or insurance agents, wants to be a financial planner."

Now, Fact Number 3: Anyone can be a financial planner. A planner need not have a high school diploma, demonstrated math skills, knowledge of pension rules or investment theory, or even much in the way of integrity. "If you decide tonight that you want to be a criminal defense lawyer, you can't start tomorrow," says Barry Vinocur, publisher of the *Investment Advisor* and the *Dow Jones Fee Advisor.* "But if you decide tonight you want to be a financial planner, you are one."

Of course, none of these three facts will surprise financial planners. But they would no doubt surprise most consumers who are looking for professional advice. After all, a plumber needs some training—as well as a license. So do electricians, lawyers, and almost every other type of professional. But a planner needs to do nothing more than print business cards. Vinocur sees the absence of barriers to entry as the biggest issue that confronts the financial planning industry. "How does it move from an industry to a profession when people can just move in and out as they like?" he asks.

Indeed, many Americans are eyeing the financial services profession as the growth industry of the 21st century. Laura Tarbox, who teaches courses at the

University of California–Irvine for people seeking the certified financial planner designation, reports that classes are heavily populated with engineers and managers who have been laid off from the aerospace industry.

"If you went back and looked at the high school yearbook, you'd find that 85 percent of the successful financial planners are those who people used to tell their troubles to."

— NORMAN BOONE

Not only is there no barrier to entry, but a planner need not do anything at all to keep abreast of legal, tax, investment, estate planning, and other developments. No surprise, then, that the media can readily find financial advisors who fall short of illustrious. In fact, most consumer complaints about advisors result from simple incompetence, rather than deliberate misconduct or fraud, according to Katherine Vessenes, a lawyer and certified financial planner who specializes in compliance issues and is author of "The Compliance & Liability Handbook for Financial Planners and Financial Service Professionals." No surprise, either, that the best planners feel they must work doubly hard to distinguish themselves from the masses of incompetent and barely competent colleagues.

Will the Real Financial Planner Please Stand Up?

A WORD HERE ABOUT HOW financial planners define themselves. Planners are *not* salespeople. While an insurance agent or stockbroker might examine a client's need for a particular product, planners take a holistic approach to the client's financial situation. They start by assessing all of the client's financial needs. Investing is just one piece of the puzzle—and it is usually not even mentioned in the first meeting, when the planner is getting to know the client. Planners like to say they help clients build better lives, rather than choose the perfect stock or mutual fund. Of course, finding suitable investments is one part of that. But so is paying off debt, refinancing a mortgage, deciding whether to accept a buyout offer. The true planner also emphasizes full disclosure of the fees and risks involved in working with him. Planners behave as fiduciaries, which means the client's needs always come first. If charged with making an unsuitable investment, a stockbroker might argue that he is not a fiduciary. But a top-notch planner never would.

The best financial planners have many things in common. Clearly, a key difference between the best and the rest lies in education and training. Yet conversations with dozens of planners did not uncover a single "best educational background" for success. Many top planners have earned master's degrees in business administration. Some of them, like Mary P. Merrill, consider an MBA "a must." But others who have an MBA—like Norman M. Boone—don't buy that. Boone goes so far as to argue that a good planner might be entirely self-taught. "If you're going to work with blue-collar clients, are you going to be better off having two years of history or English literature?" Boone asks. "That may not be as important to clients as how well they get along with you and whether you make good sense or not."

That's probably true. Key, then, are good interpersonal skills and the ability to build relationships. Broad life experiences and the willingness to translate them into a philosophy for building a sound financial life are also critical. So is the ability to listen and to hear. "If you went back and looked at the high school yearbook, you'd find that 85 percent of the successful financial planners are those who people used to tell their troubles to," Boone says. "That signifies that people trust you, that you're a good listener, and that others feel good about your common sense." It's not a skill that is easily taught. "Unfortunately, it's somewhat of an inborn quality," says Tarbox, the teacher. "We have a lot of engineers and aerospace people with excellent technical skills. They put together beautiful plans. But they wouldn't know how to communicate them to a client if their life depended on it." Financial professionals who attempt to enter planning from another specialty are often tripped up by this obstacle. "I have been working with a CPA with a master's degree in estate planning who has tried for three years to get a planning practice up and running," says Katharine McGee. "He is eminently qualified technically, but he does not have the people skills to build a practice."

The Best Educators

PERHAPS COMMUNICATING WELL with clients can't be taught, but teaching is a clear theme among the top planners, many of whom came to planning as a second career. While a finance or accounting or business degree is helpful for the technical skills, successful planners swear by what they learned from teaching. McGee, who has a degree in finance, did a stint in education when she was overseas and taught fifth and sixth graders in an American school. "There's something crucial about the educational process, about communicating concepts and ideas and helping people to learn so that the listener connects with them and remembers them," McGee says. "That's what I did as a teacher and that's what I still do with clients."

"There's something crucial about the educational process, about communicating concepts and ideas and helping people to learn."

— K A T H A R I N E   M c G E E

Virtually every planner who participated in this project had a connection to teaching, whether it was teaching children, teaching CFP courses, teaching investors—as Harold Evensky does as president of the Gold Coast Chapter of the American Association of Individual Investors—or teaching other planners, as all of them do at national and regional conferences. Jim Budros says he learns best by teaching. For the past four years, he and his partner, Peggy Ruhlin, have alternated semesters of teaching the CFP course in various subject areas such as investments, risk management, and estate planning. "You know you're representing the designation, you're representing yourself, and the firm," Budros says. "The idea of not being prepared is so frightening that I sometimes prepare more than I do for a client."

Much of a planner's education comes from broad life experience and the willingness to share it with clients, teaching them something about life. Consider Carol Caruthers, who taught elementary school and took time off to raise her children before going back to school herself to study business and, finally, to take the CPA exam at age 39. Within ten years, Caruthers headed the national financial planning practice at Price Waterhouse and, in 1995, left to run a large family office in St. Paul, Minnesota.

Although Caruthers clearly has the necessary grounding in business—she taught operations research, a discipline of applied mathematics, at the college level—it is the twists and turns in her career and the homespun advice she weaved from them that have made her a stellar financial planner. While teaching elementary school, she had several miscarriages, so she and her husband, Richard, adopted Chad and then Cara. Caruthers quit her job to spend time with Cara, who had a learning disability, and then opened a day-care center to bolster the family income. She thinks children should work. (Cara cleaned toilets for neighbors as a preteen.) And her children had the usual assortment of problems growing up. When Caruthers accepted the job in St. Paul, it was Richard's turn to make a career change. Caruthers has never hesitated to talk about the struggles her own family has had, so a client needn't feel embarrassed or ashamed to confide in her about family difficulties.

Ditto with Barbara Pope. A long-time client came to Pope when his daughter was about to marry a divorced man with two children. "He was accustomed to giving each of his children a cash gift every year," Pope says. "Now he wanted to put this daughter's gift in trust so it couldn't be used for her husband's children." Pope, who had married a divorced man with two children herself, sounded an alarm. "It's not worth alienating your daughter and getting the marriage off on the wrong foot for a couple of thousand dollars," Pope said. Her client agreed.

Good planners must acquire a healthy dose of psychology, too, and be willing to stick their neck out to apply it. Cynthia Meyers doesn't hesitate to probe when she feels there is something amiss with a client's personal life. A couple of years ago, a single female client who was about 40 called Meyers for advice on some property she wanted to buy. Although the client insisted on the purchase, her argument for buying it lacked cogency. "It didn't make any sense," Meyers says. "She kept talking about not wanting to miss the opportunity. But it really wasn't much of an opportunity for her."

Meyers discovered that the opportunity this client was really worried about missing was not owning a piece of real estate, but having a child. "I sent her to talk to a lot of single mothers and to do some research about what it would be like to have a child on her own," Meyers says. Ultimately, the client chose not to do it. "But she was very grateful for help in sorting this through," Meyers says.

How to make use of the material in your own life to teach your clients and enrich your planning? Keep your eyes and ears open. And consider Eleanor Blayney, who says that the lessons she remembers best are the ones that touch home. "Conferences are tremendous," Blayney says. "But there's a kind of suntan effect where you come out glowing with all this information, and two weeks later, you're pale again." Not so when both of Blayney's parents developed Alzheimer's disease at the same time in 1990. One of three sisters, Blayney was nearest to the family home in Connecticut and best equipped professionally to handle the chores that needed to be done. "I learned a lot in terms of gathering data in an extremely adverse situation, when people have lost their mental capacity," Blayney says. She also learned about Connecticut Medicaid requirements and living wills and powers of attorney.

Blayney's experience caused her to focus more on the issue of aging and on continuity in financial planning. "I spent yesterday visiting clients in nursing homes," she said one day in the spring of 1996. "I'm not saying I'm good at it. But it's very important to me now. As you age, the financial issues and questions get so much more difficult. I'm better equipped to deal with them." Blayney now asks new clients about aging parents, too. "Perhaps it doesn't make me technically more proficient, but it makes me emotionally more receptive," she says. "I learn best when I can get the emotional flavor of an event. That takes knowing a client, seeing them eye to eye. I do a better job when I've been in their shoes."

If she recognizes a client's situation in a seminar she attends, the material sticks with her. "I do like to attend sessions I know nothing about," Blayney says. "But if I'm frank and honest, it's the ones where I'm sitting there and names are coming into my mind that I must contact, that's when my toolbox gets full. I find my retention and my ability to carry this forward is enhanced if I have a practical application."

A Safe Place

AND NOW MEET SHARON RICH, a teacher extraordinaire. Rich taught high school before going to Harvard University for a doctorate in the psychology of education. She became involved in planning chiefly as a political outlet. As the daughter of a wealthy Houston family, Rich knew she really need not work at all. She would inherit what she needed to live on. But for her, that increased the pressure to make a contribution. She was browsing in a Boston bookstore in the early '80s when she saw a book titled, "Robin Hood Was Right." She bought it, and it led her to the Haymarket People's Fund, founded by George Pillsbury and the first of several such groups set up for "inheritors," like Rich, with the purpose of funding social change.

It was her work with the Haymarket Group that brought Rich to financial planning. "I saw that all people needed to find a safe place to talk about money and to ask questions and to be stupid," Rich says. The planning practice she set up to provide clients with that opportunity is somewhat unusual. She does not sell products. She does not receive any commission income. And she does not manage money, so she receives no asset-based fees. Instead, she is purely a fee-for-hourly-service planner. Someone might come to her for help in deciding whether she can afford to buy a home, for example.

At the initial meeting, Rich typically spends two hours finding out about a client's family, career, travel, and other goals. But then she asks the client to do all the work. "Before they come in they've done the basic homework," Rich says. "And then I send them home with an assignment sheet. They might have one to 20 homework assignments." For example, one client couldn't provide Rich with satisfactory answers about what her stockbroker was doing with her money. Rich helped this client develop a list of ten questions to ask the broker. Another client held an annuity in a retirement plan, which never makes sense. His assignment: Find out the penalty for surrendering the annuity. Another client's assignment was to check deductibles and liability coverage on auto insurance. "If I find out for them, it doesn't really teach them anything," Rich says. "This way, they're learning something, and they're not paying me to do it." In 1995, Rich reluctantly raised her hourly fee from $85 to $100 and then, in 1996, to $120 an hour. "My goal had always been to be at the bottom of the market, to be affordable," she says.

But isn't all this stuff too mushy? Is a good planner really just a good listener and a friend? No. Although they must be good teachers and communicators, planners also need the technical know-how to do the job. For starters, there is one must-have designation. That is the certified financial planner, or CFP designation, granted and regulated by the CFP Board of Standards,

Inc. in Denver. That wasn't always true. When Rich decided to study financial planning in 1983, the CFP designation was still "a mail-order course," so Rich chose instead to get a diploma in financial planning (or a DFP) from Boston University—a real school. Today Rich finds that one of the first questions every client asks is whether she is a CFP.

> *"If someone were getting into the field right now, it's hard to imagine how they could do it without a CFP."*
>
> — SHARON RICH

"It is hard to work without it," Rich says. "I have to constantly explain why I don't have it." Although Rich says she is "just enough of a rebel" to resist adding the designation, she must work hard to keep her skills and knowledge up to date. "If someone were getting into the field right now, it's hard to imagine how they could do it without a CFP," she says.

Long-time planners can pinpoint almost exactly when the CFP emerged from a group of also-rans: It was in 1995. Before that, there were a dozen different designations (*see "Alphabet Soup," page 32*). Today, serious planners must have the CFP. But that's only a start. They must also continually educate themselves. Most top planners belong to two of the four planning organizations, from which they get 50 to 100 credits per year of continuing education. Most also belong to one or two local professional and networking groups. And, of course, they attend planning conferences.

The Conference Question

THE EVOLUTION OF FINANCIAL planning from an industry driven by sales commissions to a fee-based business is clear in the changing conferences, conventions, and retreats, all of which have improved dramatically over the past two or three years. In the '80s, when the annual convention of the International Association for Financial Planning was peopled with exhibitors hawking investment products, the joke was "the bigger the shrimp at the cocktail party, the worse the product," says Deena Katz. The educational merit of the conference was marginal. "In the heyday of real-estate investment limited partnerships, I wouldn't go to an IAFP convention if you paid my way," says Jim Budros. "It was a joke."

Top planners like Budros and Katz shunned the IAFP convention, opting instead for smaller, focused get-togethers like the Conference for Advanced Planning, or CAP, sponsored by the IAFP Registry every spring in Washington, or the ICFP Retreat for certified financial planners, which was held on a college campus every summer. The IAFP's decline was exacerbated by a split in the financial planning community, with many planners dropping out of the IAFP and focusing on the Institute for Certified Financial Planners in Denver as a more professional and elite group. At the 1992 IAFP convention in Anaheim, Barry Vinocur brought the September issue of his *Investment Advisor* magazine with his cover story: "IAFP, Rest in Peace." But, whether it was Vinocur's goading or a natural evolution, the IAFP has reemerged as a contender. "Now the IAFP convention has been converted from a huckster-type affair to being, in 1995 in Seattle, the strongest program of any of the conferences," Budros says.

The challenge now in continuing education is to pinpoint the conferences that are most worth attending—or the best of a good group. Planners who used to build their annual calendar around a single event like the spring conference for advanced planning or the midsummer retreat now juggle their schedules from year to year depending on what catches their eye.

Which conferences are most worth spending time and money on? We put the question to Deena Katz, who has attended them all, spoken at most of them, and organized many, and Robert N. Veres, who reports on them for his newsletter, *Inside Information.* Veres believes that the conferences are one of the very best ways for planners to educate themselves and to pull themselves up into the ranks of the solidly successful. "The profession has evolved a de facto apprenticeship program for passing the raw ingredients of success down from the successful to the struggling," he wrote in his 1995 *Meetings Year in Review.* "It takes place around educational sessions which, themselves, seem to be several quantum leaps beyond where they were five years ago." The planners who choose to participate in the process "can move themselves into the fast lane on their career track," Veres says. "They quickly pass those who don't think they can afford the five days and a thousand bucks." If you can't attend the meetings, subscribe to Veres' *Meetings Year in Review.* It's not as good as being there. But it provides a synopsis of the best presentations.

Here is what Veres and Katz have to say about the meetings:

◆ **The Conference for Advanced Planning**, or CAP, traditionally held in Washington, D.C., in late spring and sponsored by the Registry, an elite group of planners within the IAFP, was a long-time favorite. But when the Registry was disbanded in 1995, CAP was set adrift. "Over the years, too gradually for anybody to notice, CAP had turned itself into an annual reunion of Registry members who would come together, network, and trade war stories in the hotel bar in the lobby of the

Capital Hilton," Veres wrote. The 1996 conference in Phoenix took a new tack, with three-hour workshops, including a technical presentation, a case study, and a networking session on each topic.

"For senior people, that's not very attractive," says Katz, who has been a planner for 12 years. "You don't really know who you're sitting down with and whether there's any benefit to learning what they have to say."

"I learn best when I can get the emotional flavor of an event. That takes knowing a client, seeing them eye to eye. I do a better job when I've been in their shoes."

— ELEANOR BLAYNEY

Katz, who used to be a regular, says she probably won't attend in the future. "CAP is changing a lot," she says. "It used to be attended by the crème de la crème who went to talk about advanced strategies. But now other conferences are getting better, and there is less need for CAP." Katz belongs to networking groups that fill this need for her. Veres says he found the format of the Phoenix conference puzzling. The three-hour workshops did not seem to have a natural flow, and he did not find the content useful in most cases. Stay tuned.

◆ **The Morningstar Conference**, held in late spring in Chicago and sponsored by the mutual-fund rating company based there, provides the opportunity to meet and listen to top fund managers talk about their strategies and portfolios. Until recently, Morningstar offered two different conferences, one for load funds and one for no-load funds. In 1996, the two were combined. Katz says she went to the early conferences because "we didn't have access to money managers, and it was really good to sit down with a panel of managers and talk about what they're doing." Many planners still crave the opportunity to talk with money managers face to face. But today, "a lot of fund companies are doing their own miniconferences and also teleconferencing," Katz says. Still, the Morningstar Conference has cachet. Tucker Hewes, who owns a public relations firm which specializes in mutual funds and financial planning, considers it a must. Being invited to speak is a real plum, he says. (And speakers must even pay their own way.)

◆ **The ICFP Retreat**, scheduled in high summer, evolved from a casual outing on a college campus where participants wore shorts and T-shirts to a more upscale event at a posh resort like the 1996 retreat at Grand Traverse Resort on the shores of Lake Michigan. Many hard-core planners who loved the low-key networking get-together groused about the change. But the retreat is still networking-oriented. It is an annual favorite of both Veres and Katz.

I went to my first retreat at Traverse City and thought the program was top-notch. The sessions were so good, I attended them one after another from 8 A.M. until 5 P.M. and took copious notes. It was also a great opportunity to meet people (particularly if you happen to know Veres, who knows everybody else and serves as a great link). The only drawback, according to Katz, is that the retreat has typically not permitted exhibitors. The purists have been opposed to admitting vendors. There were a handful in Traverse City, but not enough for Katz to get a good sense of what is new in the product world.

◆ **The IAFP Annual Convention**, scheduled in mid autumn, draws 1,000 to 2,000 planners, "so it's tough to network if you don't know anyone," Katz says. But in 1994, 1995, and 1996, IAFP national emerged as one of the strongest meetings of the year. Many planners said the 1995 conference in Seattle, organized by Katz and her husband, Harold Evensky, was the outstanding event of the year. Katz also likes the fact that 300 to 400 exhibitors attend the IAFP convention. "I think it's wonderful because I don't have to invite these people into my office," she says. "I go from booth to booth to see what's new. It's exhausting, but people would die to get a booth there. And I'd rather scrunch it into three days than bring 87 people into my office." In 1995, she bought the new Ibbotson database.

◆ **The Schwab Institutional Conference** for fee advisors, held in the fall either in San Francisco, where Schwab headquarters is a draw, or in a vacation spot— the Walt Disney World Dolphin in 1996—was a favorite of top planners in the mid '90s. Schwab invites only those planners who use its institutional marketplace to buy no-load funds for clients, which screens out all commission-based planners. "The material is very, very focused toward Schwab's fee advisors," Katz says. When the conference was introduced in 1991, "there weren't many good educational conferences out there," she says. Today, "the material is good. But they tend to draw from the same bank of speakers as the other meetings." Still, Schwab is a good place to network. "Schwab is very picky about who they are inviting into their institutional program," Katz said. That makes the conference a good place to meet top planners. The 1996 Schwab conference in Orlando raised some hackles, though. Many planners I talked with felt it was too lavish, that too much money was spent on food, entertainment, and on wooing planners.

◆ **The National Association of Personal Financial**

Advisors Conference, which is held in the spring, is a
favorite among many of the strictly fee-only planners
who belong. Members such as Katharine McGee and
Sharon Rich swear by this conference for both networking and educational purposes. "I fulfill many of
my educational needs through NAPFA conferences,"
Rich says. Veres, who clearly has a soft spot for NAPFA
and its mission, loves this conference, too, and says the
educational sessions are top-notch. Katz is not a
NAPFA member.

How to use these conferences? Jane King pencils in
all the conferences at the beginning of the year and
then waits to see the seminar agenda before deciding
which ones to attend. Many NAPFA members make
the NAPFA conference—as well as NAPFA regional
meetings—the core of their educational training.
Linda Lubitz attends a number of industry conferences, choosing to attend workshops in areas that she
knows nothing about, rather than going to sessions to
hone her skills in her specialities. "I know I cannot
keep on top of everything that is going on in the financial planning world," Lubitz says. "What I want to do is
find good resources so that when a situation comes up
with a client, I can go to my Rolodex or conference
book and find a place to get help."

Attacking Arcane Issues

THE CONFERENCES CAN ALSO serve as a place to meet
people with similar interests to form an ongoing study
group. For example, when Jim Budros headed a
roundtable discussion on retirement beneficiary designations and estate planning at the NAPFA national
meeting in Philadelphia in May 1995, one of the other
planners in the group suggested forming such a group
to keep abreast of these arcane issues. A mistake on a
distribution can devastate an estate, because of the 15
percent excise tax on "excess distributions" that must
be paid by the accountholder or his estate. The gov-

ernment considers distributions of more than $160,000 a year in 1997 to be "excess." If the accountholder dies, the tax is levied on his estate based on his life expectancy and his account balance. (The number is indexed.)

"We have so many clients whose assets are growing so fast in retirement plans that it's not hard for a 65-year-old to have a balance exceeding $1.2 million, which is the starting point for the excise tax," Budros says. "There are enormous liabilities for planners in this area. If you screw this stuff up, and somebody dies, and the beneficiary plan is irrevocable, somebody is going to have to pay."

Four planners including Budros; Dave Foster, a CPA and CFP in Cincinnati; Janet Briaud in Bryan, Texas; and Howard Averbach in Pittsburgh formed a group that "meets" on a conference call four times a year to explore "everything you need to know about retirement distributions." "This is a very tough area," Budros says. "And it's not tough because you're stupid. It's tough because the issues are very complex, and there are only two good sources." They are Seymour Goldberg, a tax lawyer in Garden City, New York, and author of "J.K. Lasser's How to Pay Less Tax on Your Retirement Savings" and "A Professional's Guide to the IRA Distribution Rules," and Noel Ice, a Fort Worth, Texas, tax attorney who lectures on the topic.

The study group talks about the issues of coordinating income tax and estate tax; how to use distribution schemes to maximize benefits considering income, estate, and the excise taxes; how to arrange special beneficiaries; how to use the retirement plan for charitable giving to escape taxes; and "thinking critically about how much return and how much time you need to overcome the 15 percent excise tax," Budros says. A 1996 change in the law will keep Budros' group busy over the next couple of years. Tacked onto the minimum-wage bill that passed in

August was a provision to suspend this 15 percent sur-tax for 1997, 1998, and 1999 only. That will put a major new wrinkle in planning.

One of the best known of the networking and study groups is the Alpha Group of 15 planners organized in 1990 to focus on investment management. These planners, who are scattered around the country, hold two telephone conference calls each month—one to interview a portfolio manager and the other to discuss the business of planning.

"Now the IAFP convention has been converted from a huckster-type affair to being, in 1995 in Seattle, the strongest program of any of the conferences."

— JIM BUDROS

They might talk about investments that have a neg-ative correlation with stocks, which fund managers they're hiring and firing, the pros and cons of dollar-cost averaging, and the best way to prepare quarterly reports for clients. Twice a year they get together to discuss the stuff that's too technical to talk about by telephone.

Alpha members are active in trade and professional organizations and attend a number of conferences and seminars. But they all credit Alpha as their best source of information. "It's first because it's as though you have 14 partners," says Jim Budros. "It's a wonderful exchange of proprietary thinking."

Carol Caruthers accomplishes the same thing by

serving on various boards and committees that review the most current material in the areas she most needs to know about. For example, she sat on the planning committee for the executive committee of the American Institute of Certified Public Accountants (AICPA) and currently serves on the estate and financial planning board of CCH (formerly Commerce Clearing House), the tax information service. "We have a quarterly meeting, and someone makes a presentation representing each of those areas," Caruthers says. "It keeps me up to speed on what I need to know to help clients."

What To Read?

LIKE OTHER PROFESSIONALS, planners read piles of material. But most of them still feel that it's never enough. At the beginning of 1996, Jane King made a resolution to spend one day a week reading and reflecting on issues that face her clients now and those that might come up in the future. Getting clients is no longer a problem for King and other top planners. But she wants to make certain that she continues to add value. "I've found that as my business has grown, and things get more harried, what I miss is the time to reflect," King says. "Once you have a relatively stable client base that can grow, you think: What will make the relationship ongoing, and how can I make sure I'm adding expertise?"

Most planners say they don't have the luxury of taking an occasional day to read. Still, they spend at least ten hours a week—travel time, weekends, evenings—keeping up. After the obvious—*The Wall Street Journal, Institutional Investor, Barron's, SmartMoney, Worth, Kiplinger's*—planners read *Trust and Estates,* Estate Planning from Warren, Gorham and Lamont; *The Journal of Investing; Forbes; American Association of Individual Investors Journal; Harvard Business Review; PC Magazine;* and *The Journal of Accountancy.*

Many planners swear by the information and advice they get in Veres' newsletter, *Inside Information.* When Cynthia Meyers saw the first copy in 1991, she said: "I knew this was something I needed. He had his finger on the pulse of the financial-planning nation." Veres attends all the planning conferences and provides his own insights on what's worth doing, what's a waste of time. His regular newsletters are provocative and humorous. One of the most delightful things about Veres is he is not in anybody's back pocket. And he is not afraid to criticize whatever he dislikes. Even if you don't read the newsletter, you've got to subscribe. You simply can't admit you're not on his subscription list, which includes the most illustrious planners in the business.

Planners also look for specific reads to fill in the holes in their knowledge. So it was that when Barbara Pope, who grew up as one of six children of a fireman in Appleton, Wisconsin, left the financial planning practice at Price Waterhouse to run the family office for a wealthy family in Chicago, she began looking for thought-provoking reading material that would help her to understand the mind-set of her new clients. She recommends "Children of Paradise: Successful Parenting for Prosperous Families," by Lee Hausner, and *More than Money: Exploring the personal, political, and spiritual impact of wealth in our lives,* a quarterly newsletter published in Seattle (541-343-2420).

Here are some other "must reads" for a well-rounded financial planner, complied by Cynthia Meyers, a planner in Sacramento who spends a good deal of time thinking about how to help clients find their rightful place in the world:

◆ **"The Grace of Great Things: On the Nature of Creativity,"** by Robert Grudin, who connects creativity with freedom, autonomy, and the pulse of life. "As financial planners we are artists whose expertise lies in helping people build better lives," Meyers says. "This book offers a provocative guide for designing a business that is rewarding for both planner and client."

◆ **"The Art of the Long View: Planning for the Future in an Uncertain World,"** by Peter Schwartz, offers techniques for planning your business' future as well as a guide to must-read magazines.

> *When there is a question,*
>
> *"we reimburse the client's*
>
> *account in full, automatically,*
>
> *with no questions asked.*
>
> *We do that because we think*
>
> *it's the right thing to do."*
>
> — JIM BUDROS

◆ **"The New Realities,"** by Peter F. Drucker, will challenge your thinking about our shift from a mechanical to a biological universe, the social impacts of our information society, and the move from a transnational economy to a transnational ecology. Meyers calls it "a more erudite look into the future than 'Megatrends 2000.'"

◆ **"The 7 Habits of Highly Effective People: Powerful Lessons in Personal Change,"** by Stephen R. Covey, offers "a guide for thinking about what's important in life and in business and how to integrate the two."

◆ **"Leadership Is an Art,"** by Max DePree, is full of nuggets of wisdom about leadership as well as a list of qualities that define a leader. "It will surprise you," Meyers says.

◆ **"The Armchair Economist: Economics & Everyday**

Life," by Steven E. Landsburg, maintains that economics is a tool for solving mysteries, and he shares his sense of fun with the reader. Financial planners will be interested in his explanation of why dollar-cost averaging doesn't make sense, Meyers says.

◆ **"The Rise and Fall of the Great Powers: Economic Change & Military Conflict from 1500 to 2000,"** by Paul M. Kennedy, provides an analysis of empires from the Middle Ages to the present and what led to their downfall.

◆ **"Extraordinary Popular Delusions & the Madness of Crowds,"** by Charles Mackay, reminds us that scams, manias, and deceptions are as old as history. Written in 1841, the book is a favorite of Fidelity CEO Ned Johnson.

◆ **"The New Money Masters,"** by John Train. Written in 1980, this book is a "timeless study of the investment greats," Meyers says.

◆ **"Composing a Life,"** by Mary Catherine Bateson. Sometimes successful businessmen and women miss the "beauty and art of the journey," Meyers says. Reading Bateson and "viewing life as a work in progress can bring us harmony and balance."

Getting Going

WHAT IF YOU ARE NOW A planner wanna-be? Where do you start with education and training? All of the planners who worked on this project have been in the business for a long time. They didn't start at the top. How did they get there? Many started as brokers at one of the wire houses like Merrill Lynch or Smith Barney. Some started as certified public accountants, lawyers, or insurance agents. A couple—like Sharon Rich and Katharine McGee—were always fee-only planners.

Anyone who wants to move into the elite group of planners must first become familiar with how to assess financial planning needs as well as the investment and insurance products to fill them. That usually means working somewhere to acquire product knowledge. When our planners look for someone to hire, though, they rarely look for someone from a brokerage house, no doubt because of the bias against the "selling mentality." Deena Katz says she sends prospective planners to a firm like American Express Financial Services in Minneapolis to learn the ropes. "If you're going to be dealing with products, you need to know them inside and out," Katz says. "If they go to American Express, they get to do planning. If they go to Dean Witter, they would just be brokers."

But planners can come from any field that helps them develop an inquiring mind. Before she got her MBA, Cynthia Meyers edited children's books. Meyers thinks planners must be artists who understand where the world is going in order to help their clients sculpt lives that will be successful. She reads publications like *Wired* magazine and *Mother Jones,* as well as all the standard fare. When she needed a new assistant in 1996, Meyers passed up candidates with finance and economics degrees as too narrow and hired a young man with a master's degree in music and a major in cello.

"I needed someone to fit my personality," said Meyers, who sings and acts in local theater in Sacramento. "I wanted someone who wouldn't get too bored, who had discipline, persistence, and loyalty. He practices cello five to six hours a day. Well, to me, that was a clue. And he was part of an orchestra, so he could blend."

Most planners say they look for someone who is smart "because if they're smart, you can teach them what they need to know," says Carol Caruthers. But a prospective planner must also be well adjusted. Caruthers says she's learned more from her hiring mistakes than from her successes. Her worst mistakes have been from "hiring someone who was so needy that they really needed to be taken care of themselves" or from planners who "got confused between professional and personal relationships" with clients. Today, when she hires someone who will be working on the front line with clients, Caruthers asks a psychologist to do an evaluation.

So does Charles Haines. Haines has also developed a procedures manual for his firm that helps new hires understand how the firm approaches each and every task. The psychologist Haines uses helped him see that portfolio management and financial planning are two different disciplines that require different skills. "Money managers tend to be 'thinkers' on the Meyers-Briggs evaluation, while financial planners tend to be 'feelers,'" he says. "I've restructured my practice to accommodate that." He's learned that "a financial planner needs to be more empathetic, more emotional, to be able to relate more to the client." But that personality type might not do well managing money. "You do not want an emotional person handling the portfolio," he says.

Peggy Ruhlin has a recipe for the perfect hire for her growing financial planning firm: A teacher who changed careers, became a financial planner, got a CFP, worked three years for someone else, and "then, boom, we get them." The candidate would need some marketing skills, of course, but "most of what our people do is explain concepts to clients and teach them how to be responsible for their financial affairs and how to understand investments," Ruhlin says.

That Certain Something

THE FINAL—AND MOST ELUSIVE—quality a planner must have is integrity. Perhaps integrity can't be taught. But there are some special situations that face the financial advisors who are responsible for their clients' financial well-being. "It's important for us to teach the ethics of the situations young people might face because they might be coming into something they've never encountered before," says Barbara Pope.

The most basic instruction to new hires is this: the client comes first. Financial planners are not salespeople whose loyalty belongs to an employer. They are fiduciaries who must always think first of the client. "I've had experiences with staff who will figure out how they think I want things done or what is important to me," says Eleanor Blayney. "They don't think beyond that to what the client is looking for. They're working for me and looking for my approval. I need someone who's able to see that I'm just the conduit."

For this reason, Jim Budros and Peggy Ruhlin, like many other advisors, developed a policy that any trading errors made by the firm will be resolved in favor of the client. "We feel it is one of the best ethical training grounds we can provide," Budros says. "We reimburse the client's account in full, automatically, with no questions asked. We do that because we think it's the right thing to do." But it works to the firm's advantage, as well. "It's an ethical point of view that seems costly in

On "Money"

EVERYONE LOVES TO hate *Money* magazine. "There is an industry bias against *Money* magazine because it is the most hysterical of all," says Norman Boone. Still, he reads it for self-defense. "I think you need to understand how journalists make their money," Boone says, "and you need to be able to separate out the hysteria of the investment of the month and understand that next month they will be recommending something else." But others take the high road. When a client asks Katharine McGee if she's read a recent article in *Money,* she says: "No, I don't read *Money.*" Further, she tells them: "When your subscription to *Money* runs out, why not try the *Morningstar Investor* or *Kiplinger's* magazine?"

the short run," Budros says. "But one time we got three referrals from a client in this situation because we had turned a negative into a positive for him."

"I've found that as my business has grown, and things get more harried, what I miss is the time to reflect."

— JANE KING

Still, it is a hard lesson for new advisors to learn. "One of our advisors made a trading error in a client's account that really wasn't his [the employee's] fault," Ruhlin says. "It was actually sort of the client's fault for not telling us something we needed to know." Still, Ruhlin told the young advisor: "Calculate how much money the guy lost, and we're going to write him a check." It turned out to be $352. The advisor told Ruhlin: "Actually, we underbilled him last year, and it's really not all that much money, and he'd be entirely happy if we just explained to him how it happened." But Ruhlin insisted. "There's a right way and a wrong way to do this," she told her subordinate. "We're going to write a check for $352."

REGISTERING
AS AN INVESTMENT
ADVISOR

BEST PRACTICE Do not debate about whether or not you provide investment advice, how many clients you have, or how you can escape it. Take the high road by registering with the Securities and Exchange Commission if you manage more than $25 million in client assets and with the appropriate states if you manage less.

Congress passed the Investment Advisers Act in 1940 to regulate entities that manage money for the public. This law required anyone in the business of giving advice in exchange for compensation to register as an investment advisor with the Securities and Exchange Commission. A 1997 change in that act requires only those who manage more than $25 million in client assets to register with the SEC. Those who manage less are regulated by the states.

> *"I don't think the law was drafted to apply to our type of situation. But, like it or not, we're stuck with the way the law is written."*
>
> —JOHN UELEKE

The SEC—and the states—require that financial advisors disclose their fees and procedures. They also make an effort to audit advisors to determine whether they are doing what they said they would do. Although registration—and compliance—are mandatory, they are nearly irrelevant to the quality of advice given and the level of fees charged. It seems that even the SEC acknowledges that compliance does nothing to recommend a planner by its refusal to allow those who register to list it on their business card.

Here is the rule: A person—or a broker/dealer representing several persons—who provides any type of investment advice and manages more than $25 million must register with the Securities and Exchange Commission as a registered investment advisor. This is not a credential, but a yearly renewable registration, like a dog license. The advisor is not required to qualify in any way. But the advisor must provide the SEC with a completed ADV, or "Application for Investment Adviser Registration." Part I of this form, which contains balance sheets and other financial details of the business, and Part II, which discloses what the firm charges and how it operates, go to the SEC. The SEC requires advisors to give a copy of the ADV, Part II, to a new client within 48 hours of beginning work with that client. But the SEC does not regulate the fees or the procedures that advisors outline in the form. "The filing with the SEC is really just a disclosure requirement," says Deena Katz. "It doesn't say we're any better than anybody else."

The ADV form includes the background and education of the firm's principals, the types of investments the advisors use, the fees they will charge, their method of analyzing investments, and their investment strategies. When advisors are audited, the SEC and the states want to be able to determine that they are indeed doing what they claim they will do on this form. Although the careful client might be able to learn something from the ADV, it serves no real regulatory purpose. "The SEC doesn't really care what you charge or how you do it," says Myra Salzer. "If you said you were going to charge a fee of 25 percent of assets, they would just look when they audited you to see if that's what you charged." Other planners agree. "If I say I do client reviews only every five years, then they look to see if that's what I do," Katz says.

At the time the law was written, "investment advisors" were primarily institutions like mutual funds and unit trusts that took custody of the public's money. But today, registered investment advisors include individuals who provide investment advice to other individuals. Although the act has not been updated to accommodate these financial advisors, they must comply with it nonetheless.

The Advisers Act does provide a number of exemptions or loopholes. But for the most part, trying to squeeze through them makes you look like a marginal player. For example, the law says that any lawyer, accountant, engineer, or teacher whose performance of investment services is solely incidental to the practice of his profession can be exempted. Many professionals in each of these groups eagerly claim that exemption. But the top professionals in those categories do not.

Consider Arthur Andersen LLP, the Big Six accounting firm. For Andersen, which had $4 billion in revenue in 1995, financial planning is certainly incidental in terms of revenues. But for those partners who practice personal financial planning, it is not. Financial planning is what they do with 100 percent of their time. "Rather than have to constantly explain why you're not registering, if you're serious about the business of giving advice and trying to help clients with their investment planning, then you register, and you get on with it," says Steven Weinstein, national director of personal financial planning at Arthur Andersen LLP, who helped to register that firm as an investment advisor in 1995. Amen.

Or consider Violet P. Woodhouse, a divorce lawyer in Newport Beach, California. As a practicing attorney who uses her certified financial planner designation only when she helps clients work out a settlement, Woodhouse could certainly claim the lawyer's exemption. But she does not. She registers, reasoning that when she works with a divorcing client, she will advise him or her on how to best split up the marital property. If she suggests taking the stocks and giving up the house, for example, that, to her, is investment advice. "I figure everything needs to be straight," she says. "I want to do things the right way."

Most planners do not particularly like the regulations in the Advisers Act. They do not think they were intended for financial planners or that they fit them. But they hold their nose and register all the same. Registering is taking the high road. Thanks to all the consumer information available, many clients know that planners who give investment advice must be registered investment advisors, or RIAs. They know they should ask you about it. So you either register or you spend your time explaining to potential clients why you haven't done it. "I don't think the law was drafted to apply to our type of situation," says John Ueleke. "But, like it or not, we're stuck with the way the law is written today and with the way the regulations are interpreted. We have to deal with that." Although it is not yet clear what the states will do with their enhanced regulatory duties, it is clear that they will do something. For example, there has been talk of requiring advisors who are regulated by the states to take securities exams as a test of proficiency.

Planners who have not registered might be interested to see the way Stanley H. Breitbard approached it when he was named to head the personal financial planning business at Price Waterhouse in 1983. Financial planning had always been something of an ugly stepsister in the Big Six firms. Financial planning was a service offered to executive clients. But none of what were then the Big Eight firms was registered with the SEC. Breitbard, who had a specialty in individual tax, was not a financial planner either. "This was the beginning of our thinking of financial planning as a specialty in the firm," he says. "We were thinking of it as something that not everyone can do."

Breitbard mulled over his assignment for a while. "It took me a couple of years to figure out what personal financial planning was and then to figure out how we do it in a national firm," says Breitbard, who retired from Price Waterhouse in 1995. Once he thought it through, Breitbard was quite clear that he did not want his planners to claim the accountant's exemption from registering. He believed that investment advice was the core of financial planning—and he wanted his planners to treat it as such.

"We didn't want to center on tax or estate planning or the traditional parts of the accounting world," he says. "We wanted to center our practice on investments and investment advice." And he didn't want his people to be forced to claim—as some accountants do—that they needn't register because they didn't give advice on specific investments. "That is a myth," Breitbard says. "You can get very heavily into investments without giving advice on specific investments." In fact, he says, the most important decisions are not those regarding specific securities but those concerning asset allocation. The firm's financial planners would clearly be helping clients with these decisions. And that made them investment advisors. From there, it was a very short step to deciding that Price Waterhouse must register.

"We would just be chasing our tail all the time if we wanted to rely on the accountant's exemption to avoid registration," Breitbard explains. "We'd spend more time on explaining why we didn't do it than we would on registering."

Breitbard also wanted to make a splash. "We wanted to break away from the idea of CPAs being income-tax preparers," he says. "And we wanted to be first—to get our name out as a firm that was in a leadership position in personal financial planning." When Price Waterhouse registered, "it was front-page news in *The Wall Street Journal*," he remembers.

Registering, he felt, would impose a discipline on the professionals at Price Waterhouse. Breitbard developed a set of internal procedures that dictated who at the firm did what. "We said that only those professionals in financial planning can give investment advice, and we defined that very broadly," he says. So, for example, a tax specialist could talk to a client about the arithmetic equation between a taxable and a tax-exempt bond. "But to discuss it as an investment oversteps the bounds of a tax specialist. There are dozens of types of tax-free bonds—insured, non-insured, general obligation. Only financial planners can discuss these bonds as an investment."

So for Price Waterhouse, registering as an investment advisor was part of a broad change in policy that both elevated the status of financial planners in the firm and restructured the firm's divisions to make a place for this discipline. Still, it was not simple. First, Breitbard had to get the approval of the policy board. "It consisted primarily of audit partners, who are conservative by nature and trained to be skeptical," he says. "The knee-jerk reaction was that registering would bring on more liability." That is probably the same reason that many smaller firms try to find an exemption to registering. A planner who is registered as an investment advisor has a fiduciary duty to clients to put their best interest first.

> *"You can get very heavily into investments without giving advice on specific investments."*
>
> — STANLEY BREITBARD

Breitbard was ready for that argument. "The people who are doing tax planning are to some extent giving investment advice already," he told the board. "Now we will have a controlled framework for doing this." Registering with the SEC would formalize the process and make it possible to create an infrastructure within the firm for training planners by developing practice guides and implementing quality-control procedures. "So it was not just a wild notion to get involved in a new area, but an idea that would bring discipline to something that was already a crucial part of working with individuals," Breitbard says.

Once the policy board agreed, it still took considerable time with the firm's lawyers to figure out how it would be done. The actual registration process is quite simple. But once an advisor is registered, the SEC is permitted to do routine inspections—coincidentally called audits. Although in practice the SEC does not audit many investment advisors, an audit can be time-consuming and frustrating. Those who have been audited claim that the SEC auditors all look for different things. An auditor can eat up three days' time in the office and perhaps several more in solving compliance issues. And at the time, the SEC was only the tip of the iceberg: An investment advisor was also required to register in the states where he does business, and a number of them required audited financial statements. That was a problem for Price Waterhouse because it is a private firm.

So attorneys at Price Waterhouse decided that in order to comply with the requirement to submit audited financial statements, Price Waterhouse needed to create a separate entity, which is called Price Waterhouse Investment Advisors. "It's like a derivative," Breitbard says. "It's a created entity. It only exists because we want it to exist, and the SEC recognizes its existence." Price Waterhouse outlined these plans and received a no-action letter from the SEC.

The registered affiliate does not have any employees. But Price Waterhouse gave it the power to monitor investment advice given by anyone within the firm. "That was the unique format we came up with that allowed us to register in a way that would not change our structure," Breitbard says. The registration was completed in 1987. Price Waterhouse wrote an internal manual outlining what the firm meant by investment advice and how it would be conducted. Of course, the affiliate could be audited. And it has been.

It is perhaps the fear of audits, more than anything else, that causes planners to avoid registering. "I can only speak for the small practitioners, but they're scared to death of audits and how they are going to treat the planner," says Gary Bowyer, who frequently speaks on the topic of surviving an audit. "You can get hit by two different auditors that will go after completely different things."

Perhaps because Price Waterhouse is in the business of doing audits, Breitbard was not overly concerned. "But we took it seriously and they did, too," Breitbard says. "When they audited us at Price Waterhouse, they had several instructions." For example, Price Waterhouse was storing client files off site. The SEC wanted them on site. The SEC also required that the planners sign conflict-of-interest documents that said they were not investing in client securities.

"They wanted to make sure we had a policy in place and that we were monitoring it regarding personal investments that our planners make and that they're not in conflict with clients," he says. Breitbard pointed out that CPA firms have very stringent independence rules that they must follow. "But that wasn't good enough for them," he says. "So we had to institute a procedure of having our people submit their personal stock and other investment transactions."

Over the past decade, Breitbard, who served as head of the personal financial planning division of the AICPA, has become a vocal advocate of registration for accountants and has pushed accountants to give investment advice. "I tell them, if you say you're doing financial planning, investment advice should be a central part of your practice," he says.

When CPAs back away from giving investment advice, Breitbard believes it hurts the profession; when they are not seen as experts in investments, it hurts the profession; when accountants who practice as financial planners send their clients out to an investment advisor for investment advice, it hurts the profession. "That says that CPAs cannot be full-fledged financial planners," Breitbard says, "and all of that is bad for our profession."

The State Debate

GIVEN THAT INVESTMENT ADVICE is key to implementing a financial plan, why do so many planners avoid registering? In her "Compliance and Liability Handbook," Katherine Vessenes reports that when the International Association for Financial Planning polled members to see how many were registered, just 51 percent of those responding said they were. And just 64 percent of the certified financial planners who responded said they were registered. Most avoid it because of the fear of audits. Or simply because they don't want to waste time with the complexity of filing and updating a registration. And many planners believe there is not a penalty if you don't.

"We would just be chasing our tail all the time if we wanted to rely on the accountant's exemption to avoid registration."

— STANLEY BREITBARD

The SEC certainly isn't going to send anybody after those advisors who don't register. It doesn't even have the staff to monitor and audit those who do register. And there are disclosure requirements that spook some planners. Others argue that because they are not taking custody of assets, the law was really not intended to apply to them. Many, of course, take the professional exemptions. And some claim an exemption because they have only a minimal number of clients.

For example, a planner who acts as consultant to a family business or a family office might claim that he has only one client.

Perhaps the chief reason that planners avoid registration is not because of the SEC, though, but because dealing with the states can be such a nightmare. There are no common laws. It's like state income taxes: each state has different rules. Some require that advisors pass certain tests—like the Series 6 or Series 7 securities tests—before they register. Acceptable test scores vary from state to state. Some states require bonding. Others exempt advisors from registering if they have a minimum number of clients.

Some states don't require registration at all. For example, Myra Salzer, whose practice is in Colorado, is not required by that state to register. But she is in the process of registering in Texas because she has a Texas client. She can add one client in California and two more in the state of Washington before she must register in those states.

And laws frequently change. For example, one of John Ueleke's large clients moved to Massachusetts some years ago. There was no requirement for registration at the time. But the law changed. "All of the sudden we found ourselves out of compliance," Ueleke says. "We had to get a letter of exception from them because we were not soliciting any new business." Many states, though, do not have any exceptions. "So if you have a client who moves to one of those states, you are faced with the dilemma of either firing the client or going through the headaches of the registration process," Ueleke says.

Ueleke faced a quirky situation in his home state of Tennessee, too. When he became a fee-only financial planner in 1982, he still held a brokerage license. He registered with the SEC. But Tennessee would not permit him to register as an investment advisor while he held a brokerage license. The state maintained that registering as a broker and as an investment advisor was dual registration.

Ueleke had a conversation with the state securities commissioner. "He realized we had a problem," Ueleke says. "But he said he didn't know what to do about it because that is the way the law reads. He told me as long as we kept our noses clean, they wouldn't bother us." Still, Ueleke spent plenty of sleepless nights before he finally gave up his securities license and was able to register a couple of years later. "Then we had to go back and plead leniency because we hadn't registered," he said.

Inconsistent Nitpickers?

THE INTERNATIONAL ASSOCIATION for Financial Planning asked William R. Meck, head of the Securities and Exchange Commission's audit program for registered investment advisors in the Northeast, to speak at the Conference for Advanced Planning in May 1995 about who needs to register. "If you're in this room, you should be registered," Meck flatly stated.

But, given the SEC's odds, you are unlikely to be audited. It has only 60 examiners devoted to financial-planning offices. They conducted 1,000 audits in 1994. With 22,000 registered investment-advisor offices, that works out to about one audit every 22 years.

If you are one of the unlucky ones, you are unlikely to be audited by anyone who is knowledgeable. The turnover is so high that Meck described an auditor with three years' experience as a grizzled veteran. "We have people with just two to three years in the field training others," he said.

So it's not surprising that planners who have been audited, like Gary Bowyer, fuss that SEC auditors are inconsistent nitpickers. "You never know what they're going to ask for, because they don't know either, and

The states are not only the most troublesome in terms of registering. They are also the most likely to find advisors who have not registered. "The SEC does not have much of an enforcement arm that is reaching out to try and find people who are not registered," Breitbard says. "But the states have been very active in that regard." For example, Breitbard knows many CPAs who have gotten "show cause" letters from the secretary of state or some other state authority asking why they haven't registered. "Maybe they see an ad in the yellow pages, or they see an article

no two of them ask for the same thing," Bowyer says.

Meck claims the SEC is looking for evidence of fraud or theft from clients. "If you're fair to your clients, then you have nothing to worry about from us," he said.

The largest issue on the auditor's agenda is whether the planner takes custody of client assets. "If you're going to steal, then custody is 90 percent of the game," Meck told the group. "If you really can't get at the money, we're a lot more relaxed around your office."

The auditors also look for evidence that the registered investment advisor is using some type of instrument to look at client profiles and determine suitability; evidence of churning, if there are any commissions involved; and self-dealing, or buying and selling for their own accounts in advance of buying and selling for the client.

The auditor will, of course, look to see how you charge fees or commissions and whether you have properly disclosed that. "Always, we're going to look for whether you disclose it up, down, and sideways," Meck said.

someplace saying that this person is a financial planner or that they were giving a speech on investments," Breitbard says. They follow up.

There is probably a planner somewhere who need not register as an investment advisor. But it's not you. Good financial planning involves a heavy dose of investment advice. It may not be the most important aspect of financial planning. But it is certainly critical. If you want to play a part in elevating the practice of financial planning, you owe it to the profession to register and to comply with all the state laws. You can mount whatever argument you like for not doing it, but the fact of the matter is that it makes you less professional. Increasingly, consumers will ask if you are a registered investment advisor and will want a copy of your ADV.

> *"The knee-jerk reaction*
>
> *was that registering would*
>
> *bring on more liability."*
>
> — STANLEY BREITBARD

It's true that registering does little to keep marginal planners out of the business. Nor does it elevate the level of planning done. Marginal or incompetent advisors simply practice without registering. "The intent of the legislation is not to pass on the merits of the advisor," Weinstein says. In fact, the intent of the securities laws in general have nothing to do with merit. It is disclosure to the consumer that is the foundation of the securities laws. The notion that an educated consumer is an informed consumer requires that everything be disclosed. The disclosure of how fees are charged and how investment strategies are devised goes to the heart of that. That starts with the ADV that is filed with the SEC and provided to clients. The best advisors in the business register. Period.

CHAPTER

DISCLOSING
FEES &
RISKS

BEST PRACTICE Lay out the details of how you do business and all of the costs involved. Follow up with a written summary and ask the client to sign and return it.

In her "Compliance and Liability Handbook," lawyer Katherine Vessenes points to the failure to disclose fees and investment risks as one of the most common areas of consumer complaints about financial professionals. "It is not uncommon for clients to seek to be reimbursed their entire investment because they were not advised there were sales charges," Vessenes writes. As in other areas of planning, though, there are few guidelines on how advisors should disclose their fees—or even on how much or what kind of fees they should charge.

Deciding how to charge fees is largely up to the planner. Traditionally, consumers bought financial products from a salesperson who earned a commission. In the mid '80s, there were only a handful of financial planners who charged fees rather than commissions. That has been changing rapidly in the '90s as the words "fee-only" before "planner" emerged as something of a merit badge in the media and with consumers.

> *"We view financial planning*
>
> *and portfolio management*
>
> *as two distinct businesses.*
>
> *We don't expect that a client*
>
> *will hire us to do both."*
>
> —TIM KOCHIS

Fees are touted as a cleaner way of doing business, with less potential for the conflict of interest inherent in commissions. "I don't think a human being can operate [on commissions] without thinking as much about his wallet as about his client's financial security," planner Robert Ayres in Naples, Florida, told *Investment Advisor* magazine. Many planners say there was a "sea change" in their thinking when they moved from a commission-based to a fee-based business.

Fees are clearly the future. Many fine planners still use commissions, though, and unfortunately, they have been made to feel like second-class citizens. When Cynthia Meyers made the case for commissions in an article in the *Dow Jones Investment Advisor*, she says, "I got calls from so many people thanking me for being so brave." But obviously integrity doesn't depend on the type of compensation received. "Converting from commissions to fees doesn't change you," says Harold Evensky, who changed his practice to fees in 1991. "I'm still the same person. You either put the client's best interest first, or you don't."

The 55 planners interviewed for this book set fees in a variety of ways, and there is a case to be made for each one. Here are some of them:

ASSETS UNDER MANAGEMENT Like many other planners, Harold Evensky charges an annual management fee based on a client's assets. Fees are 1 percent of assets up to $1 million, 80 basis points to $3 million, and negotiable over $4 million. (Evensky's minimum is $1 million. Other members of his firm manage smaller accounts based on model portfolios developed by Evensky.) The firm charges a fee of $1,000 to $2,000 for developing an investment policy for a client. The client is free to take the policy statement elsewhere or to implement it himself, if he likes, rather than hiring the firm to manage his assets with no-load mutual funds. Evensky, Brown, Katz & Levitt is chiefly an investment management firm and does not do comprehensive financial planning. The firm does not receive commissions from any products at all.

FLAT FEES Some planners charge an annual retainer for all planning work. For example, when he first meets with a client, Bob Willard sets an annual fee that is based loosely on assets under management, but also includes such factors as whether the client is equipped to trade electronically; whether the account is with Charles Schwab & Co. (which makes it easier for him because he can download it on his computer) rather than with a full-service broker; and a range of other considerations. For Willard, that fee stays roughly the same. He argues that managing a client's affairs actually gets easier as he gets things in order. Further, a good

client brings him other good business. One client started out with a fee of $24,000 several years ago and now
pays $36,000, even though he "was barely a millionaire
when he started" and is now a multimillionaire.

Andy Hudick uses a similar system, setting a fee for
the first year that covers the time it will take to develop
a comprehensive financial plan. It is a dollar amount
rather than a percentage. At the beginning of the second year, he sets a lower fee because the bulk of the
work is already done.

COMMISSIONS Cynthia Meyers believes that commissions are more fair for the client than fees. "I'm suspicious about the trend to assets under management,"
Meyers says. "I think it's more expensive for the client.
And I think it can result in the planner putting his
interest before the client's." Meyers says she chooses to
receive her compensation from load funds for three
key reasons. First, she believes annual fees piled on top
of the fund-management fee make investing too
expensive for the client. Second, no-load fund companies don't send her the statements she needs to track
performance. Third, she worries that clients will be ill-
served by putting their money in no-load funds that
include a lot of "hot money" from inexperienced do-it-
yourselfers. If they jump ship in a market downturn,
the portfolio manager might be forced to sell at the
wrong time to raise cash for redemptions.

Meyers acknowledges that she sometimes feels that
the tide is moving against her. But, she says, "that's the
way things are now. The tide will turn when clients
start to question whether they are getting value for
their annual fees."

FEES PLUS COMMISSIONS Like Evensky, Ross
Levin charges an asset-management fee of 1 percent
of assets. But he is not a pure fee planner, chiefly
because insurance plays an important role in Levin's
practice, and he is not happy with any of the no-load
disability and life-insurance policies available. So when

a client needs an insurance product, Levin's firm collects a commission.

FEE OFFSET Some planners who are in Levin's position elect instead to charge a fee and to offset that fee with commissions when they are forced to use a product that is structured with a commission. Many planners, like Lynn Hopewell, used fee offset as a transition on the road toward fee only.

STRICTLY BY THE HOUR Sharon Rich does not sell products. She does not manage assets. She collects an hourly fee for the time she spends with clients. Period. In 1996, she reluctantly raised her fee from $100 to $120 an hour. Like many purists, Rich is a member of NAPFA, which does not permit members to accept commission income.

FEE BY FORMULA Bert Whitehead's average client is a middle-American family with a household income of $100,000 that needs the full gamut of planning, from budgeting, cash flow, insurance analysis, and college saving to retirement planning. A client might want to know what type of mortgage to get or whether to buy or lease a car, for instance. Whitehead says he tried asset-based fees but came to believe they represented a conflict of interest. For example, if a client needed to make a decision about paying off a half-a-million-dollar mortgage, the paydown could reduce his annual fee by $5,000. Likewise, if a client wanted advice on whether to leave his 401(k) money with the company or roll it into an IRA, the decision would affect the amount of assets under management—and thus Whitehead's fee.

Now his fees are based on a formula that takes into account income and total net worth with "a factor built in for complexity." A typical first-year fee is $6,000. The renewal fee, which includes preparation of tax returns, is based on total net income and assets. "Our renewal range is $500 to $3,000, with an average of $1,500," Whitehead says.

HOURLY FEES PLUS ASSET-BASED FEES Bob Wacker combines the compensation systems of Sharon Rich and Harold Evensky by doing some hourly fee planning and some investment-management work. Wacker charges a one-time fee that might be as low as $2,400 for a comprehensive financial plan. He will also do an investment review and make investment recommendations for as little as $750. "That would be a case where we're not going to be monitoring it on an ongoing basis," Wacker says. "That makes it affordable for someone with $20,000 or $30,000."

He has no asset minimum for managing money, but his minimum annual money-management fee is $1,200, considerably lower than most fee planners'. "I think my services are fairly priced," Wacker says. "Once you've done a plan and implemented it, I don't know much you can add in value." Wacker aims to keep the total cost to clients under 150 basis points—including his own fees and the fees they must pay to the mutual fund company. Wacker, too, is a NAPFA member.

Likewise, Marilyn Capelli charges fees for two separate services. The first is financial advisory services, primarily comprehensive financial planning, which she has done since 1981. All of her clients are financial planning clients. She will not accept anyone who wants only investment management. Initially, she made recommendations on investments as part of her comprehensive plan and left it up to the client to implement them. But she found the client typically didn't follow through.

"We would get together for our next semiannual meeting, and a lot of times, the things we'd discussed hadn't been done," she says. So in 1995, she added an investment advisory service. For a small additional fee, she handles the recommendations herself, making certain that mutual funds are purchased or sold and that changes are made. She puts client portfolios in an account at Schwab so that the client gets a single statement, and she can monitor it more easily.

FEE CAP Like Sharon Rich, Mike Chasnoff is a fee-only planner and a member of NAPFA. But in addition to hourly fees and asset-based fees, Chasnoff estimates how much time he will spend on a financial plan and then tells the client the maximum he will charge. For clients who prefer a retainer, Chasnoff estimates how many hours he will spend and then caps his fee at that upper end of the range. "But we have a little special arrangement that says our total retainer expense cannot exceed ½ of 1 percent of the assets in their investment portfolio," he says. Minimum assets under management: $400,000.

"I don't think a human being can operate [on commissions] without thinking as much about his wallet as about his client's financial security."

— ROBERT AYRES

CONVERTING TO FEES Hundreds of financial planners are converting their compensation from a commission-based to a fee-based business. And thousands more would like to—or will be forced to by the brokers that employ them—within the next couple of years.

There are three primary motives for converting, according to Bert Whitehead, who set up a company called Cambridge Advisors to offer workshops on the transition. The first is that planners on commission are getting squeezed as no-load funds and no-load insurance become readily available. Second, Whitehead says, is that much of America's wealth sits in 401(k) plans, and few commissions are earned on this money. Planners must also perform financial housekeeping tasks that are not covered by commissions.

Third, "there's a recognition that fee-only is the higher ground," Whitehead says. Although commissions people obviously believe they do the best they can for clients, it's still the difference between being in sales and being a fiduciary with the client's best interest at heart.

The problem with converting is that it can take a long time to build sufficient cash flow from fees. But Whitehead claims his workshops can cut the time significantly. "The conventional wisdom is that it takes three years to convert," Whitehead says. "We've been able to condense it to three to six months."

Whitehead says he set up the business because so many planners had approached him for advice on making the transition. "One of the biggest obstacles to going fee-only is the lack of a system," he explains. His program includes education in all aspects of financial planning, a software package, workshops, intern time, and coaching. The cost is $10,000.

ADV, Plus

HOWEVER THEY CHOOSE TO charge for their work, top planners believe in full disclosure. They consider the ADV required by the Securities and Exchange Commission to be only a starting point for disclosure. For some planners, like Cynthia Meyers, the ADV, Part II, is filed by the broker/dealer that handles their transactions. (A broker/dealer is the only type of business that can legally sell securities. They can range in size from Merrill Lynch to a tiny shop that serves only one financial planning office.) In Meyers' case, the broker/dealer is Foothill Securities Inc. in Los Altos, California. The ADV filed by Foothill covers all the fees and procedures of the planners that sell securities through this broker/dealer. So Meyers' clients do not learn a great deal about her through this document.

To fill the void, Meyers includes a section in her financial plan disclosing the commission she receives on mutual funds. "If I recommend moving an individual retirement account to American Funds, I do a blurb on the funds, and then I always say: 'There is a 5.75 percent sales charge on this investment,'" Meyers says. She also mentions the breakpoints, or the dollar investment required to qualify for a lower sales charge. "I say, 'If you invest $50,000 in American Funds, there will be a reduced charge of 4.5 percent,'" she says. And she makes clear to clients that they will pay a higher commission by using several different fund groups.

She does not, however, disclose "trailing commissions," or the annual fees of 25 basis points or so that many fund companies pay to brokers for keeping investors in their funds. Even so, she goes much further than many commissioned planners. "When I tell other planners what I do, they're horrified," Meyers says. Sometimes her candor backfires, too. For example, she recently met with a client who studied her disclosure statement and decided that he was paying too much. Meyers argues that because she chooses funds with low expenses—chiefly the American Funds, with expenses of around 70 basis points—and keeps her clients invested for the long term, her total fees are lower than those of many fee planners.

As a commission-based planner, Meyers is in the minority among elite advisors. Some, like Levin, are waiting for good no-load insurance products before completing the transition to a fee-only practice. But most agree it is inevitable. Consider what superplanner Nick Murray, author of a number of top-selling books for financial planners, including "Serious Money" and "Gathering Assets," writes in the May 1996 issue of the *Dow Jones Investment Advisor*: "I'm operating under the assumption that before too long, commissions will be a vestigial remain (like the little leg bone in the dolphin's fin), and we'll all be working for an annual percentage of assets, which I think is most likely to settle out around 1 percent."

Even the wire houses are following this trend, albeit sometimes reluctantly. In 1995, Merrill Lynch, Prudential Securities, and Smith Barney announced that they would move to no-load funds. Many industry observers, like Robert N. Veres, editor of the industry newsletter *Inside Information,* expect to see a business that is largely fee-based by the year 2000.

> *"I'm suspicious about the trend to assets under management. I think it's more expensive for the client. And I think it can result in the planner putting his interest before the client's."*
>
> —CYNTHIA MEYERS

Yet Veres acknowledges that he expects few planners to offer the strictly-by-the-hour fees of a Sharon Rich or the formula fees of a Bert Whitehead. Most planners will be somewhere in the middle, with a combination of hourly and asset-based fees. This complexity of fees makes disclosure a complicated issue. For example, if an advisor charges an annual management fee to manage a portfolio of mutual funds, should he disclose the additional fees charged by the mutual funds themselves? Yes. "I lay out every single dollar they pay for everything," says Bob Wacker. "Sometimes the client gets bored and doesn't want to hear any more.

But I make them listen to everything." That includes fees charged by a discount broker, which most advisors use for convenience, too.

Value-Added Disclosure

DISCLOSURE OF FEES AND SERVICES is a critical first step in signing on a new client. Adequate disclosure serves the advisor as well as the client. If the fees are unclear, the client might have cause for complaint later. If the fees—or the planner's minimums—are higher than expected, the client may be unprepared to pay them. Planners who have substantial minimums for new clients want to make certain the client is qualified before wasting the time of either planner or client. "It's very important from a business standpoint to know what your thresholds are for doing business and to be very clear about them to prospective clients," says Tim Kochis. "If the client is not prepared to spend that amount, then he should go elsewhere, and you should help him find someone else if you can." Here are some of the ways planners disclose their fees, and at the same time qualify clients.

REWRITING THE ADV Some planners rewrite the ADV, creating a brochure that makes the turgid information required by the SEC more accessible to clients. There are a couple of drawbacks to this approach. First, the brochure must be revised each time there is any change in the way you do business. For some planners, an annual revision is adequate. "But we find that we're changing ours all the time," says Deena Katz. "That means we'd have to be reprinting the brochure constantly." The second problem is that an SEC auditor may decide that the brochure does not meet the disclosure requirement because it does not include everything that is in the ADV, Part II. For example, David Diesslin successfully used such a brochure through many SEC audits until, in January 1996, an auditor told him it didn't meet the requirement.

Diesslin now sends new clients the ADV and a separate marketing brochure.

Bob Wacker has surmounted both these obstacles. He uses a brochure that is a friendlier version of the ADV. It is not the glossy, four-color document that we think of as a brochure. Instead, Wacker prepares what he calls his "Registered Investment Advisor Disclosure Statement," discussing his services, fees, the types of clients he serves, the way he makes investments, and his educational background, then stores it in his computer and reprints it each time he needs to update it. The document is much easier to digest than the SEC form. When Wacker was audited in October 1995, the SEC did not find any problems with Wacker's brochure. "They said the brochure does, in fact, include everything in the ADV, Part II," Wacker says. Although the brochure helps a client understand what he does and how he gets paid, it is still pretty dense. Nor is it designed to woo new clients. "No way is it a marketing brochure," Wacker says.

THE ONE-PAGE FAX When Tim Kochis gets a call from a prospective client, he speaks to him briefly over the phone and asks for a fax number. "Then we send them what we call a 'one-page scope-of-services document,'" Kochis says. "It goes into as much detail as you can put on one page, indicating how we do our business, how we are compensated, our fee threshold, and our portfolio-management threshold so that we can quickly use this to qualify prospective clients." Like many planners, Kochis has separate minimums for financial planning work ($4,000 based on hourly fees) and for portfolio management (a floor of $1 million in assets). The fax "serves two purposes," Kochis says. "It gets the initial disclosure out right away. It tells them what we do, how we get paid, what our fee threshold is. And it also qualifies them. If they don't meet the threshold, they're not going to bother to call back."

THE PHONE SCREEN Bob Willard screens out what

he calls the ABCs, or "affluent but cheaps," over the phone. "In the early days, I put an ad in the yellow pages and responded aggressively to every call and analyzed every situation," Willard says. But experience taught him that good clients never came via the yellow pages. Now he outlines his fees over the phone when a prospective client calls to avoid wasting anyone's time. "I tell them that there's no point in charging them a dollar to save 50 cents," he says. Willard emphasizes that he makes this a friendly conversation. "If I can answer a quick question for them, I'll do so pro bono and wish them the best of luck," he says. "Or if it's a client that one of my associates would be comfortable with, that's fine." But there's no point in spending a lot of time and sending out required disclosure material to a client who is a poor fit for his practice, he says.

THE MARKETING BROCHURE This is where the planner tells the story he wants to tell to woo the client. Because the press and much of the public view fee planners in a positive light, most emphasize that in their brochure. "We emphasize the fact that we are a registered investment advisor but, because we are a CPA firm, we cannot, under California state law, take commissions," says Stan Hargrave, making the firm, in a sense, above the fray. "But even if you are compensated by commissions in part, there is a very positive story to tell about your form of compensation and all the other good things about a firm, including the tenure of their people, the experience, the education, the kinds of clients they serve, the kinds of specialization they have," Tim Kochis says. "It's possible to put all the things required by disclosure in a very positive light."

Kochis has developed a 25-page marketing brochure for this purpose. But he rarely uses it for individuals. "For them, once they get the one-page document, they're presumably sold," he says. The larger brochure, which goes into great detail about the investment process, is saved for presentations to corporate sponsors or law firms that want to hire planners for their executives.

THE PINK SHEET Because the principals at Evensky, Brown, Katz & Levitt are often quoted in the national media, the firm gets lots of calls from prospective clients. This is a double-edged sword. It's nice to be noticed. But many of the callers are not a good fit for the firm, which does only investment management, not comprehensive planning.

The solution, developed by Deena Katz, is called the pink sheet because it's printed on pink paper. When a client calls, Katz chats with him on the phone and fills out a client-qualification form. It includes questions like: What do you think we can do for you? "Everybody has some type of agenda, and that's when I decide whether they're appropriate and that's when I tell them our fees," she says. If the client isn't a fit with the firm, Katz tries to refer him to someone else or, if it's a quick question, to answer it pro bono.

But she keeps the pink sheets and adds the names to the firm's database. Everyone gets the firm's newsletter for six months. After six months, she sends prospective clients a form asking whether they would like to continue receiving the newsletter. Sometimes a prospect will come back two or three years later, this time understanding what the firm is about and ready to sign on for investment management. "It's kind of like an elephant having a baby," Katz says. "They've finally decided they want to do business with us, and I can pull out these pink sheets and I have copious notes on our first conversation."

THE CHAT Most planners do an initial face-to-face meeting at no charge, but only after they have screened the client to be certain there is a potential fit between client needs and advisor services. This is usually a get-to-know-you meeting where advisor and client agree on what services are necessary and on fees. At this meeting, planners typically discuss the various fees a client will pay to do business with them. For those who do comprehensive planning, the first meeting typically focuses on planning tasks rather than investment tasks. "We view financial-planning work and portfolio management as two distinct businesses," Kochis says. "We don't require or even expect that a client will hire us to do both." This first sit-down also gets financial planning fees on the table.

> *"You have to sell the risk and*
> *not the benefit, because*
> *everybody is really listening to*
> *the benefit and not the risk."*
>
> — V I O L E T   W O O D H O U S E

Planners who specialize tend not to offer the freebie meeting up front. For example, Violet Woodhouse, a lawyer and planner who specializes in divorce, says she never does. "People know what they want when they come to me," Woodhouse says. "All of my time is spent delving into the facts and helping them walk through the analysis."

THE ENGAGEMENT LETTER After the initial meeting, Elaine Bedel sends out an engagement letter outlining the five or six planning tasks that were discussed and giving the client an estimate of the fee. With this letter, she sends ADV, Part II. "Most of the disclosure information has probably been discussed in that first meeting sitting in the office," Bedel says. "I talk about my background, how I practice, and so on. But I don't really have the ADV on my desk, pointing things out."

THE INVESTMENT-POLICY STATEMENT An unhappy client can always claim later that he was never informed about the risks inherent in an investment. Financial planners emphasize that there are many different types of risks in investing and many obstacles to achieving financial goals. Perhaps the most significant ones are that a client will neglect to put away enough money or fail to invest aggressively enough to keep pace with inflation. Yet from the client's point of view, risk means just one thing: volatility, or the risk of loss of principal. Will my dollar ever be worth less?

The challenge for the advisor is to lay out these various risks so the client understands them. If the client does not see that his investment may fluctuate in value, he may bail out of the investment plan when the market goes down, guaranteeing that he will lose money.

How to determine how much risk the client can handle? Elaine Bedel says she believes that clients come to her to assess their risk and that there is little point in asking the client to do a self-assessment. "They look to the planner to help them determine how much risk they can take," she says. "We talk about the ups and downs of the market, but I tell them that's the only place they're going to have growth, and if time is on your side, that's the best way to reduce risk."

David Diesslin uses a risk questionnaire to determine how much financial education a client has and what their expectations are. "The mistake I commonly see made by investment advisors is that they expect the client to identify where they are in the investment-risk spectrum," Diesslin says. "That assumes that they have one, and we just have to find it."

No matter how much or how little risk a client seems ready to take, failure to disclose those risks is dangerous. "If you don't disclose the risk, and you don't get it in writing, you are going to be subject to some sort of suit," Woodhouse says. "You have to sell the risk and not the benefit, because everybody is really listening to the benefit and not the risk." Woodhouse suggests providing a glossary that identifies all the fees and the risks involved in investing in mutual funds and asking the client to initial it. "You must make it clear to them that a dollar in may or may not be a dollar out," Woodhouse says.

Stan Hargrave, who specializes in representing financial advisors in lawsuits, agrees. "If you are ever asked by a judge how you determined the level of risk and you say, 'I had an informal discussion with the client, and I made some notes,' it is better than doing nothing, but it doesn't carry a lot of weight inside of a courtroom," Hargrave says. "But if you present a form that shows you asked questions that were answered in detail in the client's own handwriting—and not just 'yes' and 'no' but essay answers—that is an 800-pound gorilla in the courtroom."

When the risks of investing have been discussed, the planner lays them out—in writing—in the investment-policy statement. Many planners illustrate the volatility risks in the portfolio by showing the client the historical outcomes or one and two standard deviations. The investment-policy statement also discusses asset allocation, selection of money managers, performance ratings, and expense ratios.

THE ACTION PLAN When a client decides to implement the investment policy with Evensky, Brown, Katz & Levitt, he is presented with an action plan. "Then we plug in the actual funds and talk again about all the fees associated in investing in mutual funds," Katz says. "We talk about the different costs of portfolio management, and we talk about brokerage fees and custody fees and money manager fees and mutual fund expense ratios and advisor's fees, so they understand where everything comes from." She lists the specific funds that she recommends and what the expense ratios are and "every bit of information we could possibly toss at them."

Is this too much information for the client to digest? Perhaps. But advisors say they do it anyway. "One of my problems is that I go to such lengths to disclose everything that it probably confuses people," Wacker says. "But I will still continue to do it." For example, Wacker tells clients that he uses Charles Schwab & Co. when he manages their money. But he points out that if he were to buy a fund from the Vanguard Group or T. Rowe Price & Associates through Schwab, it would cost the client more than if they bought it directly from the fund company. "I lump all these things together along with my fees so that they can see the total they're going to be paying on a percentage basis," Wacker says. "I

Surviving an Audit

THE SECURITIES AND EXCHANGE commission claims it doesn't have enough staff to adequately audit the registered investment advisors who offer financial advice to consumers. Yet nearly all of the advisors we talked to had been audited. They offered some procedures that can help make an unpleasant experience go more smoothly.

◆ **Don't submit to an audit on the spot if it means you must postpone essential client meetings or other business.** "You don't have to screw up your whole day because the auditor appears at 8 o'clock in the morning," says Jane King. "You can reschedule, and if you want your lawyer with you, you can certainly have that." Don't get indignant about it, though, lest the auditor think you have something to hide. Politely ask to reschedule.

◆ **Don't try to anticipate what the auditor will focus on.** It's always something different, says David Diesslin, who has been audited several times. "Each person is looking for something different, as well as the issue du jour from the commission," Diesslin says.

◆ **Develop a compliance manual that outlines pro-**

think it's important that they see where everything is coming from. I never want a client to come back and say: 'Gee, am I paying the portfolio manager, too? So what am I paying you for?'"

THE SIGN-ON Clients who are signing up only for financial-planning tasks sign and return the engagement letter with a deposit. Those who want investment-management services are required to initial a statement acknowledging that they have been shown all the fees involved in the investment portfolio and that all risks have been outlined.

cedures for your shop. "That takes care of two thirds of the things they are looking for right off the bat," says Bob Wacker. "It also helps with training new people in your firm to follow the right procedures."

◆**Don't apply logic to the SEC requirements.** For example, several advisors who use mutual funds for client accounts said they hadn't developed a formal insider-trading policy for their firms. "We didn't see how we could move the market by buying SoGen Fund," says Deena Katz. But when her firm was audited in the summer of 1995, she discovered that the SEC always looks for insider-trading documents. Now Katz has each member of the firm turn over monthly brokerage statements to one of the principals, who reviews them and stamps them. In addition, each employee has signed a statement saying, "I know what insider trading is, and I won't do it."

◆**Assign one person in the firm to work with the auditor.** This partner should find the auditor a place to work and ask him for a list of documents he wants to see. "You don't have to let them rifle through your files," says Stan Hargrave. "You can bring them what they ask for." *(continued on next page)*

THE FOLLOW-UP New clients often need lots of handholding, particularly if they are inexperienced investors. Jane King makes regular calls to new clients. "You just can't communicate with them too often to say, 'Well, now your dollar is $1.02, or now it's 98 cents, and here's why, and here's what's going on,'" King says. The frequent communication helps clients become comfortable with the stock market. "They're much better able to understand the risk they're taking, and maybe even turn it up after six months or 18 months, because they start to see how it works," King says.

◆ **Make certain that you have the files to back up the fees and procedures you have filed in the ADV.** "The SEC is looking for disclosure," Katz says. "They're looking to see if you do business the way you say you do business."

◆ **Don't get too anxious.** An audit may be annoying and time-consuming. But this, too, will pass. "There is not a lot they can do to you unless there is fraud involved," Katz says. "There is really no right and wrong to the fees you charge and the way you operate your business." You simply must have the files to prove it.

When Eleanor Blayney's financial planning firm was audited by the Virginia State Corporation Commission at the end of 1994, Blayney decided to see what she could learn from the process. "I wanted to see what business practices we could improve so that not only would we be better prepared for audits, but also for our business," Blayney says.

Here are some of the things she focused on:

◆ **Retrievability of information.** "We knew all the information was there, but it hadn't necessarily been

"The mistake I commonly see made by investment advisors is that they expect the client to identify where they are in the investment-risk spectrum."

— DAVID DIESSLIN

rationalized," Blayney says. As a result of the audit, Blayney created a system with both permanent files and ongoing working files. "We color-coded the permanent hard-files differently," she says. "We also created in the computers different files for every client so all the correspondence is filed in the computer file."

◆ **Centralized compliance information.** Blayney appointed one person to do all the compliance work, including the filings with all the states where the firm has clients. "We're working at the intersection of three jurisdictions—Virginia, Maryland, and D.C.— and we have to register with every state," she says. Further, as the firm's clients retire and move south, the firm must register in many other states as well.

◆ **Reexamination of contracts.** "It forced us to look at our contracts again to make sure that they clearly specify all the essential things, such as a termination provision," Blayney says.

◆ **Investment plans.** Blayney added a page where the client signs the plan, acknowledging the agreement on how assets will be managed.

4

ACCEPTING A FIDUCIARY ROLE

BEST PRACTICE Put your client's interest first in every respect and act as if there is no question you are more concerned about his money than about how much money you make from him.

"This will be a short chapter," says Andy Hudick. "You are a fiduciary. That's it. End of chapter." He's right. If you don't want to accept fiduciary responsibilities, get out of financial planning. Financial planning is just now on the cusp of becoming a real profession, thanks to the efforts of a number of hard-working individuals who are setting standards to elevate the level of competency and integrity of those who practice.

Planners at the top of the profession accept the label without comment. Many of them—like Jack Blankinship—include it in their marketing brochures.

But another contingent of planners is still attempting to sneak out from under the label because it carries too much liability for their taste. "Too many people still want to duck it," says James Wilson, who fought to have the word "fiduciary" included when he helped write practice standards for the International Board of Certified Financial Planners in 1992. Wilson lost that battle because the bulk of the group wasn't ready yet. "Financial planners want to be a profession, and yet they don't want to pay the price to be a profession," says Wilson. "They want the goodies. But they don't want to pay anything for them."

To Wilson, a fiduciary relationship means that you have a client rather than a customer. "You owe the duty of a merchant to a customer," Wilson says. "You have a duty not to defraud. But you have no duty to protect. With the client, you owe a duty to protect." Webster's definition of a client is "one under the protection of another." Planners are fiduciaries whether they like it or not, Wilson says, because they get to know clients and then offer investment advice tailored to specific situations, casting them in a fiduciary role.

Wilson recalls that a surgeon once told him that one of the reasons surgeons are paid so much is because there are a lot of physicians who have the training and skill to practice as a surgeon, "but we actually do it," the surgeon said. "When I start cutting, I'm either right or I'm wrong. And that's that. But you can't get the benefits of being a surgeon without cutting." So it should be with planners, Wilson says. If you're going to give investment advice and collect the money for doing it, then you've got to accept the responsibility.

Indeed, that is the way it would look to consumers if they understood this controversy. They don't, at the moment. "No one has ever asked me if I'm a fiduciary," says Lynn Hopewell. That's largely because consumers don't understand the distinction between a customer and a client. But they will when business reporters start adding it to the recommended checklists that magazines are always drawing up for how to find a financial planner. And that's probably not such a bad idea. Consumers should be getting advice from someone who has promised to put their interests above his or her own and is willing to take the responsibility for it.

> *"You owe the duty of a merchant to a customer. You have a duty not to defraud. But you have no duty to protect. With the client, you owe a duty to protect."*
>
> —JAMES WILSON

Those who look strictly at the legal definition of a fiduciary will claim that this is unfair. They will claim that planners sometimes act as fiduciaries and that sometimes they do not. And that the circumstances dictate whether a planner is a fiduciary. Fiduciary does have a legal meaning, of course. "It is somebody who has responsibility for somebody else's money," says Lynn Hopewell. Obviously, a trustee or the executor of an estate is a fiduciary. "A fiduciary must put the client's interests first in every respect," Hopewell adds.

But even from this strictly legal point of view, planners fit the definition, according to the research Deena Katz did on this topic for a number of articles she wrote about fiduciaries. Katz believes the notion of who is a fiduciary is changing to include financial planners. Here is what Katz says: Beginning in 1974 with the Employee Retirement Income Security Act (ERISA), then in 1992 with the Third Restatement of Trust and in 1994 with the Uniform Prudent Investor Act, there has been a paradigm shift in the standards applied to investing as a fiduciary.

For example, the Code of Federal Regulations, Title 29 Labor, defines a named fiduciary as "a person who renders investment advice...as to the value of securities or their property or makes recommendations as to the advisability of investing in, purchasing, or selling securities or other property," Katz wrote in the January 1996 issue of *Financial Planning* magazine. "Note that the code refers to giving advice or making recommendations, designing investment policies or portfolio compositions, or creating diversification," Katz says. The "or" is significant, she says. "You don't have to perform all of these duties to be considered as a fiduciary under ERISA, and the relationship need not be in writing. Nor must you be named in the plan document to be a fiduciary. You just have to have assumed the responsibility of acting in the interest of the plan."

That, Katz says, sounds like a planner. "If you are a planner providing investment advice for a fee, you probably begin the engagement by creating an investment plan or policy and outlining the objectives and needs of your clients," Katz wrote. "This document probably contains a list of current investments, as well as a proposed asset-allocation strategy, illustrating to the clients that diversification of the portfolio will help them attain their stated goals. You also may include an implementation or action plan, again outlining how a repositioning of the assets will improve the portfolio." Many planners also use a brokerage firm like Charles Schwab & Co. or Jack White & Co. to hold the assets and take discretionary authority over them.

Katz says many planners object that these things apply only to advisors who work with employee benefits plans, not to those who work with individuals. But, she points out, "Black's Law Dictionary" describes a fiduciary relationship as "one founded on trust or confidence reposed by one person in the integrity and fidelity of another." Based on this research, Katz believes it is clear that planners are fiduciaries.

If the law doesn't say it now, it soon will. She sees adopting the title as a defensive measure and added it to her firm's brochure. "Just because I don't like that label doesn't mean I'm not going to have the liability," Katz says. "So I see a left hook. If you lean into it, maybe the impact isn't so hard."

Many other planners—like Gary Bowyer and Andy Hudick—say that simply registering under the 1940 Investment Advisers Act, as all those who give investment advice are required to do, makes you a fiduciary. "Everybody who gives advice or who holds himself out to be a financial planner in any way, shape, or form comes under the 1940 Advisers Act, and they are, therefore, a fiduciary," Hudick says. "If you as a consumer or client hear them say something other than that, you should run."

Filling out the ADV makes it clear that anyone who registers is a fiduciary. "The ADV guides and manual that tell you how to fill out the ADV use the word 'fiduciary' any number of times in explaining how to do it," says Blankinship. "Those rules say that anybody who accepts compensation for advice is a fiduciary."

Whatever line of reasoning they use to get there, top planners do not quibble about the language. "The way I feel about my clients, I am embracing the fiduciary role," says Barbara Pope. "What I want is whatever is in their best interest, and I feel that responsibility—and that guilt—morally, if not legally." As a consumer, I would rather go to a planner like Pope or Blankinship than one who is trying to duck the label. I would reason that if a planner is willing to take that responsibility, he must be confident in his competency. And he must have my best interest at heart.

So why would a serious planner argue that he is not a fiduciary? To avoid the liability that goes with it, of course. "If you had a lawyer advising your firm, he would probably tell you: Don't be a fiduciary if you don't have to be," Hopewell says. "If you say you are a fiduciary, you undercut your defense."

> *"Just because I don't like that label doesn't mean I'm not going to have the liability. So I see a left hook. If you lean into it, maybe the impact isn't so hard."*
>
> — DEENA KATZ

The part about lawyers is certainly true. In fact, when Wilson was campaigning on the issue in 1992, one of the other committee members brought a lawyer to a board of governors meeting to tell the planners why they should not add the word to the code. The lawyer made two arguments against it, according to the minutes of that meeting. Both had to do with liability. The legal burdens of proof are substantially different for fiduciaries, he said. If a planner is not a fiduciary, then the *client* must prove that the planner did something improper and that the client was injured in some way. But if the planner operates in a fiduciary capacity, then the burden of proof shifts to the planner to prove that he operated openly and honestly with the client.

The second reason brought up by the lawyer was that if a planner operates in a fiduciary capacity and does not do proper disclosure, a client can sue and have the contract for fees voided, even if he profited from the advice. I guess that argument supposes that some planners might forget to operate openly and disclose fees and other procedures. Yet they would still want to be paid for their work. That might be hard to explain to a client—oops, customer.

When Wilson took his fiduciary fight on the road in 1992, Thomas Watterson of *The Boston Globe* attended the meeting Wilson conducted in Boston. Watterson was not impressed with the proposed Code of Professional Responsibility, which did *not* include the word fiduciary. "Financial planners like to say they are professionals, like accountants, lawyers, physicians, or architects," Watterson wrote in his column in *The Boston Globe* on May 7, 1992. "But after reading the proposed Code of Professional Responsibility, it looks like most of them still see financial planning as a more complicated way to sell life insurance."

Watterson found one of the most curious parts of the proposed code to be its distinction between 'client' and 'customer.' A client was described as "someone who enters into a relationship of trust and confidence with a personal financial planner," but the words 'trust and confidence' did not appear in the definition of a customer.

The intent was "to distinguish those situations where a planner creates and implements a full-blown financial plan for a client from cases where he or she simply responds to a request from a customer to buy one product, like a mutual fund," Watterson wrote. Jack Blankinship explains that some planners—he was not among them—wanted to be able to do consulting work for clients without gathering all the data that makes a planner a fiduciary. "If a client comes into a planner's office and asks, 'Do I have enough money to go on this cruise?' or 'How much money should I put down for this new home?' there could be a lot of work done for that person without being held to the fiduciary standard," Blankinship says, although, as he points out, he would not be willing to answer those questions for the client without gathering more information—and becoming a fiduciary.

Eliminating the words 'trust and confidence' is a way of helping planners who do not wish to become fiduciaries, Watterson wrote. At Blankinship's firm, "we've

Process Particulars

ACCEPTING THE FIDUCIARY LABEL means you must also have a process in place to help you make investment decisions. And you must document it. The Uniform Prudent Investor Act of 1994 is a parallel of ERISA, according to Donald Trone, author of "The Management of Investment Decisions," one of the best books available on this subject. "It means all clients can be treated the same: trusts, individuals, pensions," he said. "As you manage the investment decisions, be sure to document the process, hire competent professionals, and always, always remember you work for the participant/beneficiary," Trone told the planners at the ICFP Retreat in summer 1996 who attended his seminar on the Uniform Prudent Investor Act. There are a number of steps in the investment process, each of which must be completed and documented, Trone said. He provided planners with this:

1 Time horizon: What is the length of time assets can be committed? Trone splits that into two time frames. Five years and over is long. Under five years is short.

2 Asset-class preference: What asset classes will

decided not to answer a question until we've developed financial statements and collected all the information we need," he says. Then they are able to enter into a relationship of trust and confidence with the client. "But it would be possible to answer a question without getting into investment advice," Blankinship says. "There are a lot of people who do that. So they argue they're not fiduciaries."

What about the argument that accepting the label of fiduciary weakens your defense if you must ever go to trial? Blankinship dismisses that. "We say in our

---

be considered? For short-term investors, only fixed income is appropriate. "So there's no asset allocation," he said.

3 Allocation: Allocate assets to each asset class.

4 Sub-asset classes: Consider manager strategies or styles.

5 Choose a money manager or mutual fund to manage each specific asset class or strategy. "This is the least important decision you have to make," Trone said.

To meet his fiduciary obligations, an advisor must first prepare written investment-policy statements and document the process he used to arrive at the investment policy, Trone said. "You're not judged on performance. You're judged on the process. Your clients are hiring you to bring discipline, reason, and rigor to the investment process."

Second, he must diversify assets with regard to the risk/return profile of the client. "If you are providing cookie-cutter asset allocation, you are not meeting the requirements," Trone stated. When one planner objected that the overwhelming majority of asset allocations end at 60 percent *(continued on next page)*

brochures and firm documents that we are fiducia-ries," Blankinship says. "People say that we are hand-ing somebody a loaded gun, but we don't think so." Blankinship reasons that he is following all the rules, all the best practices, abiding by the prudent investor rule, completing an investment policy statement, doc-umenting everything. "That's why I don't mind just say-ing: 'Look, if I'm taken to court—and I hope to never be, of course—but if I'm taken to court, I'll give them that card. They don't have to prove that I'm a fiducia-ry because I do all those things. So let's just have at it.'"

Clearly, the top planners believe that it is in accept-ing the label of fiduciary that they set themselves

stocks/40 percent bonds, Trone agreed. But he emphasized that you can't start at 60/40, you have to arrive there by going through a process. "It's true that most end at 60/40. But we can show how we got there. If a client doesn't have a strategy, they will do the wrong thing at the wrong time."

Third, the planner must use professional money managers or prudent experts. To choose a mutual fund or money manager, Trone said you should look at six areas:
- performance numbers
- performance relative to the risk assumed
- performance among peers
- adherence to style
- performance in rising and falling markets
- the key decision-makers and the tenure of the managers. "What I hang my hat on now is the or-ganization," he said.

Fourth, you must control and account for all expenses. "If you use load funds, you have to be able to justify it," Trone said. "That's hard." Fifth, you have to monitor the actions of the money manager. And

apart from those who simply sell financial products. "It's very difficult, if not impossible, for registered reps to stand in a fiduciary role that calls for them to hold the client's interest first, because they owe their first allegiance to their firm," Blankinship says. They have dual interests. And they have a loophole. "The broker gives customers ideas, and they can say yes or no," says Norm Boone. "But they are as free to say no." But a financial planner—or registered investment advisor—is exploring with the client goals and objectives, time horizon, and risk tolerance in order to help the client develop a financial plan. And then the planner tells the client which investments to use

sixth, avoid all conflicts of interest.

Trone uses the acronym RATE to stand for what he considers the most important thing in the investment-policy statement. RATE stands for the four asset-allocation variables you should consider—risk tolerance, asset-class preference, time horizon, and expected return.

When Trone works with clients on risk tolerance, he tells them: "I have no quiz. If you want a quiz, call Merrill Lynch." Instead, he looks at three things: the projected returns on an asset class, the projected levels of variation or the standard deviation, and the projected correlation of asset classes.

He tells the client: If you want zero loss, you need 80 percent fixed income and 20 percent equity. That gives you an expected return of 6.6 percent. Will you be happy with 6.6 percent? Most clients, of course, say they would not. They want 10 percent. To get 10 percent, Trone tells them, you need almost 100 percent equities. He tells the client: "Almost all clients have a mutually exclusive risk and return limit. You have to give something up."

in the plan. That makes the planner a fiduciary.

Just because a planner refuses to accept the label of fiduciary does not mean that a court will not see him as one. "Rejecting the label doesn't mean I won't have the liability," says Deena Katz. "He can call himself whatever he wants," adds Bob Willard. "He can pretend he's not a fiduciary. But if he goes to court, he's going to be a fiduciary. It's black and white. People feel that they can hide themselves from legal exposure. But they cannot."

"Everybody who gives advice or who holds himself out to be a financial planner in any way, shape, or form comes under the 1940 Advisers Act, and they are, therefore, a fiduciary."

— ANDY HUDICK

And, of course, just because a planner chooses an investment that goes down in value doesn't mean he will lose a lawsuit. Your defense is in documenting why you chose the investment and in proving that you explored the client's needs and determined that this was a suitable investment. If you are already doing that, you needn't be so worried. "Fiduciaries have been successfully sued for neglecting their duties and for not doing their job and for being incompetent," says Lynn Hopewell. "But nobody has ever successfully been sued simply for losing money, provided he followed a prudent process."

That makes documenting all client contacts critical. Andy Hudick does a follow-up letter after every meeting with a client. "I do it because it's easy to forget things," he says. "I write down everything we decide, and they just get a one-page letter with bullets, saying: 'We agreed on the following things: You're going to do this; I'm going to do this.'" Barbara Pope takes notes while she's on the phone with people, dates them, and sticks them in the file.

And finally, even some of those planners who are adamant about their fiduciary role maintain that there are some situations where they are not fiduciaries. Those are situations, chiefly, where the planner is not in control of the investment decisions and the process. For example, if a planner is hired as a consultant to a 401(k) plan, he is likely to emphasize that he is a consultant, not a fiduciary.

"Accepting fiduciary responsibility also means knowing the people you're representing," Katz says. "You may be once removed from that because you're consulting to the plan administrator or the plan trustee."

Katz has done consulting work for pension plans where she called herself a consultant and didn't make certain decisions that she would make with her clients because she hadn't met the plan participants. "It was not our responsibility to educate them," she says. "It was our responsibility to advise the plan administrator." Blankinship agrees. "We purposely do not take on a relationship where we are not in complete control," he says. But when you are meeting with clients, delving into their personal situation, talking about risk, goals, and so forth, and then giving investment advice, "you better get used to the F-word," Katz says.

CHAPTER 5

CONFLICTS OF INTEREST

BEST PRACTICE Eliminate every possible
conflict and lay the rest of them on the table.
Take particular care in detailing how you are
compensated. Mention every wrinkle, including any possible advantages you gain from
doing business with particular vendors.

Compensation is the most obvious conflict for financial planners. And that conflict
is most obvious in commissions. In the
1980s, when salespeople racked up high
commissions for selling limited partnerships and products that were underwritten
by the firms that employed them, most of
them didn't breathe a word about what they
were making.

Many Wall Street firms pay brokers more to sell in-house products. Or they offer a bigger trailing—or annual—commission for keeping customers in these funds. They push brokers to unload their inventory. And most brokers and insurance salespeople don't discuss their compensation with customers. Indeed, many are offended by the suggestion that they should. But top planners who use commissions disclose exactly what they earn. They provide percentage figures as well as total dollars. And they mention the trailing commissions they collect, money given to them simply because a client remains in a fund or insurance product that they sold.

Hourly or percentage-based fees harbor conflicts, too. "If you charge hourly fees, how do I know that you won't take twice as long to do the work as you should?" asks Ross Levin. If you charge clients based on assets under management, there will be many times that you will give advice that will result in higher fees for you. Every one of them should be disclosed to the client.

"The relationship you have with a client is really serving two interests," says Violet Woodhouse, "and so there is an inherent conflict."

Coming Clean

YOU MUST IDENTIFY ALL THESE conflicts to the client in writing so the client is in a position to question your conduct and to know what the alternatives are. "You lay it out in writing so they understand that there is a conflict of interest in your recommendation," says Ron Rogé. "Then you tell them what your recommendation is, and you point out that your fees will be higher if they follow your advice."

But compensation is certainly not the only conflict. "This whole industry is riddled with conflicts," says Ross Levin. "It's a question of how many hairs does it take to make a beard."

Financial planners spend a lot of time trying to distance themselves from stockbrokers and insurance agents. There are a number of reasons for this. But the most basic one has to do with conflicts of interest. Salespeople inevitably serve two masters: the customer and the firm—or the customer and themselves.

> *"The relationship you have with a client is really serving two interests, and so there is an inherent conflict."*
>
> —VIOLET WOODHOUSE

Top financial planners put the client first. But the distinction has been muddied by the armies of stockbrokers and insurance agents who have begun to call themselves financial planners or financial consultants. Some estimates put the number of people who call themselves financial planners at around 300,000. But there are approximately 32,000 people who hold the certified financial planner designation. Perhaps a third of them are what we think of as *real* financial planners.

That leaves the real planners with an identity crisis, which largely explains the growing strength of the fee-only contingent. In the 1990s, planners began using "fee-only" to signal that they were financial advisors—fiduciaries—who put the client's needs above their own and that they would advise the client on all aspects of financial well-being—on overall wealth building or wealth management.

Although there is nothing about charging fees that changes a person, charging fees is a more straightforward way of disclosing conflicts, planners say. And many planners maintain that something changes in their practice as they move from commissions to fees. "There's a recognition out there that fee-only is the higher ground," says Bert Whitehead. "Although most commissions people I talk to believe in their heart that they treat clients fairly, all of them have been amazed at the paradigm shift that happens when they go fee only. It's the difference between being a salesman and being a fiduciary."

One group, in particular, has distinguished itself by charging fees rather than commissions—and really made an issue of it. That is the National Association of Personal Financial Advisors, or NAPFA. NAPFA has very strict rules for membership. Those planners who join must not use any products that provide a commission. They are permitted to continue to receive trailing commissions from mutual-fund sales that were made before they converted to fees, although this sometimes creates practical problems. For example, a planner must be affiliated with a broker/dealer in order to receive trailing commissions. Some broker/dealers do not wish to be affiliated with planners because of the liability involved. And if a planner holds any type of securities or insurance license, he is not permitted to join NAPFA. For example, Bob Winfield holds an insurance license that he has used only twice in the last several years—once to sell a policy to himself and once to sell one to one of his best friends. "But that's enough to keep me out of NAPFA," Winfield says. Planners must also submit a financial plan for review if they wish to join NAPFA.

There is considerable tension between NAPFA members and other groups who use only fees. In the roundtable discussions I conducted as research for this book, tension sometimes flared between NAPFA members and those who don't qualify for membership—or those who have chosen not to join. Some planners believe that NAPFA members have fostered a holier-than-thou attitude for promotional reasons.

Some planners, like Tim Kochis and Harold Evensky, refuse to buy into the notion that the label "fee-only" alone puts you in an elite group. "Frankly, that's the reason I haven't joined NAPFA, even though I qualify," says Kochis, a lawyer and fee-only planner who has held a number of leadership roles in the profession. And, of course, many planners are simply envious of NAPFA members because they, for one reason or another, have not been able to let go of the vestiges of commissions and securities licenses that would enable them to qualify.

The resentment will not be reduced by NAPFA's successful move in 1997 to get a service mark on "fee-only." Bob Willard, one of the members behind this secret initiative, says he heard the *Investment Advisor*'s Bob Clark address a NAPFA group in the mid '90s and tell them that they had won the battle over fees versus commissions. Fees were now recognized as the high road. But, Clark warned them, they still might lose the war, because planners of all stripes would simply call themselves "fee-only."

That got Willard to thinking. He and a handful of other NAPFA members, like Ron Rogé, began to work on the service mark. It took more than two years. As part of the project, NAPFA and the Consumer Federation of America sent a "mystery shopper" to planners in the Washington, D.C., area who called themselves "fee-only." A full 58 percent were not true fee-only planners, Rogé said. In January 1997, NAPFA announced the survey results and its service mark.

NAPFA chairman Mark Spangler said the only appropriate use of the term fee-only now is when a financial advisor is paid directly by and only by the client, and when there are no commissions involved. Spangler said a commission has been appointed to determine how to monitor and enforce the service mark.

NAPFA has only 300 fee-only members, with another 200 or so associates. But they are a powerful, highly visible group of dedicated professionals. Gary Pittsford was one of the original NAPFA members. Pittsford, who was once a stockbroker with Equity Funding, started his fee-only firm in 1973. Like most NAPFA members, Pittsford sees the move from commissions to fees as the difference between night and day. "I wanted to be fee-only and charge like lawyers and accountants," Pittsford says. "There were just a few other people who did that at the time. None of us knew each other."

> *"Although most commissions people I talk to believe in their heart that they treat clients fairly, all of them have been amazed at the paradigm shift that happens when they go fee-only."*
>
> —BERT WHITEHEAD

These pioneers started making contact and arranged a meeting at the annual national convention of the International Association for Financial Planning in 1974. "The fee-only people agreed to have breakfast together at the IAFP meeting," Pittsford recalls. "So we'd have our own little miniconvention." This tiny group grew from ten in the late '70s to 75 by the early '80s, providing a core group that was big enough to organize a separate meeting for fee-only planners.

In 1982, the group piggybacked its own meeting of 100 fee-only people on the IAFP meeting in Atlanta. "We had a little nucleus of hard-core people by now,"

Pittsford says. "In 1983, we incorporated a company called the National Association of Personal Financial Advisors." Pittsford was the first president; his hometown lawyer in Indianapolis incorporated NAPFA and drew up all the papers in Pittsford's office. By 1997, NAPFA had its own national convention and a nucleus of fee-only people, some of them zealots.

NAPFA by no means includes all the planners who qualify for membership. In fact, many of them—like Kochis—will not join because they are put off by NAPFA's position that they stand alone on the high ground. Others, like Marilyn Capelli and Charlie Haines, have joined only recently after years of practicing as fee planners.

For example, Capelli, who has been a fee-only planner since 1981, joined in July 1995. "I really felt that NAPFA was too single-minded," she said. "I chose to be fee-only because it fits with my philosophy. But I know too many ethical people paid by other methods. It bothered me that NAPFA was so zealous." But over the past few years, she felt that NAPFA was "widening its horizons." She's delighted that she joined. "It has been a wonderful source of referrals and information," Capelli says. She particularly enjoys the e-mail conversation where various NAPFA members ask questions about regulations, tax changes, new laws, and other issues. "I go into the e-mail every day, and usually, I learn something," she says.

Pittsford acknowledges that NAPFA established an early reputation for zealotry. It hardly seems surprising to me that such a group would choose to distance itself from the corruption and conflict that was rampant then in limited partnerships and such. "In the '80s, there were eight or ten radical people," Pittsford says. "But all those people are basically washed-out now. Most of those who are left appear to be levelheaded."

There are still plenty of true believers, though, like Ron Rogé, who heads the public relations committee for NAPFA. Rogé believes—and rightly so—that NAPFA members go a long way toward eliminating conflicts with full disclosure of fees and procedures. And, not surprisingly, he trumpets that benchmark to the press. Rogé has done a masterful job of getting reporters to believe that fee-only planners in general— and NAPFA members in particular—are a cut above the rest of the ranks.

Pressure Zones

HERE ARE SOME OF THE SPECIFIC areas of conflict that our planners are concerned about:

1. HOW MANY ASSETS UNDER MANAGEMENT? There has been a clear trend over the past several years for planners to charge asset-based fees for financial planning services. Many planners do some hourly consulting work with a new client to set up a plan and then charge an ongoing fee based on a percent of assets under management. Or they charge a flat fee for the up-front work and then convert to a fee based on assets under management. That fee is typically around 1 percent, although many are higher. Clearly, anything that causes the client's assets under management to change affects the planner's compensation and it should be disclosed. Here are some sticky ones:

◆ **401(k) assets.** Many clients have a large chunk of their assets in the company 401(k) plan, particularly as they approach retirement. Many planners do not consider 401(k) assets to be part of their investment assignment. Some charge a flat fee to help a client make an allocation decision. Others, like Judy Shine, charge nothing to set up a static asset allocation for the 401(k).

As the client approaches retirement, he must make a decision about leaving the money in the plan or moving it to an individual retirement account. If it is rolled into an IRA, 1 percent of it might go into the planner's pocket. If it stays in the company plan, the planner gets nothing.

"Let's say your 401(k) is $300,000," says Gary Pittsford. "I do not charge you anything extra while you are an employee. But if you roll it over, it is considered assets under management."

Pittsford has several clients between ages 65 and 70 who have retired from employers who permit them to leave their 401(k) money in the company plan. Helping a client make that decision presents an obvious conflict for him. Of course, he must make an objective decision about what is best for the client. But he must also disclose—in writing—the conflict between his interest and the client's.

Other planners, like Charlie Haines, have restructured their business in a way that eliminates this conflict. Haines had been charging a flat asset-allocation fee for providing advice on picking investments for a 401(k) plan. "We discovered through our time analysis that it actually took more time to handle the 401(k) assets in the asset-allocation process and in performance reporting," Haines says. "So here we were charging less for something that was actually more costly to deal with." Fees were revised so that the 401(k) plan assets are now part of the assets under management.

◆ **Buyout offers.** Clients with buyout offers from their employers present the same potential conflict. If the employer offers to sweeten the retirement package and gives the employee the choice of taking a lump sum or an annuity, the planner who charges an asset-management fee clearly earns more if his client takes the lump sum.

But there are often advantages to leaving the money with the employer and taking an annuity. It might be difficult for a planner to match the employer's investment return. Many employers subsidize retirement payments. For example, they might offer a sweetened survivor benefit to the spouse. Or they provide cost-of-living adjustments. Sometimes the employer offers retiree medical benefits only to those who choose the annuity option.

"We had a client in that situation several years ago," says Bob Winfield. "We saw that there was no way we were going to be able to earn what the company earned. Plus they offered a cost-of-living adjustment. We advised the client not to take the lump sum."

But a planner who advises the client to take the lump sum must lay out the conflict as well as his reason for recommending the lump sum.

◆ **Debt.** The same conflict exists with debt. It's pretty clear cut with credit-card debt. If a client comes in carrying credit-card balances at 16 percent, paying off the debt is a no-brainer. But what about a mortgage at 8 percent? Should he start saving and investing or pay off the mortgage? Traditional wisdom dictates that mortgage debt is part of good tax planning. You go for the most expensive house you can manage and let Uncle Sam help you pay for it via the tax deduction for home-mortgage interest. But many planners don't buy that anymore. The tax reform bill of 1990 limits all deductions for upper-income taxpayers. That means they're not getting much tax relief for paying mortgage debt.

So Ron Rogé, for one, advises his clients to pay off the mortgage before starting an investment program, even though it means his fee will be lower. "Let's say the client comes to you with a half-a-million-dollar mortgage, and they have a half-a-million-dollar portfolio, and they ask if they should pay down the mortgage," Rogé says. "When you do the analysis, if you're going to tell them not to pay down the mortgage, you have to disclose to them that if they keep it in the portfolio, and you're going to manage it, that's part of your fee. Then it's up to the client to make the judgment call as to whether your analysis was good or whether you were just trying to keep the fee."

But Rogé says he finds that it's usually beneficial for

his clients to pay down the mortgage. "So that ends the discussion right there," he says. Rogé says he has a number of Wall Street traders who are in very high income brackets as clients. "They don't even know their tax deduction is phased out," Rogé says. "So we just basically have them get rid of the mortgage and start saving once the mortgage is paid off."

> *"Making a mistake on a $10 million account is an 'oops'. But making a mistake on a $1 million account could drastically change their lifestyle."*

— MYRA SALZER

Myra Salzer, who works with inheritors, faces another twist on this issue: Many of her clients join the firm with all their assets in the stock of one company that was started by a grandfather. "They probably carry the stock at a zero basis," Salzer says. "If we sell the stock and diversify them, they have to pay capital gains, and there is less money under management." But, clearly, diversifying is the prudent thing to do. So Salzer typically charges at the lower rate to begin with.

2. WHERE TO PUT YOUR TIME? Planners say they sometimes wonder just how much time it takes to do a top-notch job for a client. How do you know you're giving them what they're paying you for? What is enough? "I can always spend more time with a client," says Myra Salzer. "So the conflict for me is: How much should I do? How many times should the trust document be reviewed? Should it be checked with other attorneys? To what extent do I go to really provide the service they're paying for? That's a personal conflict."

Salzer also wonders how many clients she can take on and how complicated their financial situations can be without sacrificing something essential. "There can be months in there that are very, very easy," Salzer says. "But then you have two divorces, three deaths, a marriage with a prenuptial agreement that you have to deal with all of a sudden. You can't time these things. You have to be available. So who knows what is the right number?"

Allotting time amongst clients is tough, too. "Do I give a $1 million account as much attention as a $10 million account?" Salzer asks. Because she charges fees based on assets under management, she earns much, much more from the $10 million client. But the $1 million client might suffer more if he doesn't get enough attention. "Making a mistake on a $10 million account is an 'oops'," Salzer says. "But making a mistake on a $1 million account could drastically change their lifestyle."

Most planners acknowledge that they face a conflict in dealing with clients who are difficult. It's easy to put the more likable clients first. For instance, on one particular afternoon, when Andy Hudick had phone messages from ten clients and only a few minutes to return calls, he picked the two he liked best. "I knew they wouldn't call me unless they had something to ask, they wouldn't waste my time, and I could answer their questions," Hudick says. Of course, he also called the other eight back before the day was out. But it's only natural to prefer dealing with those who are easier to deal with.

Like other conflicts, planners acknowledge this one—to themselves and maybe to each other, but not in writing to those pesky clients—and strive to be fair.

3. WHAT TO DO ABOUT SOFT DOLLARS? Expensive golf outings and vacations paid for by vendors are clearly a part of compensation. And they must be disclosed in the ADV. Top planners handle that by avoiding them. However, some planners do make due-diligence working trips to visit mutual-fund companies. Or, in the case of the Alpha Group of planners, they invite vendors to speak at their meetings and charge them a fee—of perhaps $1,000 or $1,500—for the privilege. All of these seemingly mundane exchanges of dollars must be disclosed, too.

"Soft dollars to pay for a marketing seminar must be disclosed," says Bob Winfield. "Even though the client was not harmed in any way, and even if the advisor received no gain, it still has to be disclosed in your ADV. The SEC will hold you accountable to those standards."

Judy Shine used to think that was going too far. Shine says she took the position that if she went on a working trip to visit a mutual-fund company, for example, and the fund company picked up part of her expenses, she was simply doing a good job for clients and keeping her expenses in line, which helped her keep her fees lower.

But a conversation with Mark Spangler, a Seattle planner, at one of the national conventions persuaded her that she was wrong. In mid 1996, she wrote a letter to clients informing them that she makes occasional due-diligence trips and telling them which fund companies have paid part of the tab. "Most clients were really surprised about the letter," Shine says. "They couldn't see the conflict."

Now it is clear to Shine. "It might be a conflict of interest that is in my client's favor, because when I sit down and talk with money managers, I feel I do a better job for them," Shine says. "So I'm not going to stop doing it. But I do want my clients to know it's there. If they have a problem with it, they can talk with me about it."

Ron Rogé handles this by including a de minimus rule in his ADV. For example, Rogé believes it is acceptable to have lunch or dinner with a vendor when the vendor picks up the tab. But that's about it. "Somebody told me that the best policy is that you have to be able to eat it or drink it within a two-hour period," Rogé says. "So you can use that as your de minimus rule."

4. WHAT DO YOU GET FROM CHARLES SCHWAB & CO.? WHAT DOES SCHWAB GET FROM YOU?

Many fee planners use Schwab as a back office for their client accounts. They get a free hookup to Schwab and discounts on client trades. They also get streamlined statements, a broad variety of mutual funds, and good service. In fact, it isn't much of an exaggeration to say that Schwab had a big role in creating financial planning as we know it today by allowing planners to freely use mutual funds from dozens of different companies—as well as institutional funds and load funds that can be obtained at net asset value. Schwab also gets something, of course. Fees at Schwab are higher than at some of the other discount brokers like Jack White & Co. But the client pays those fees, not the planner.

So does the planner use Schwab for the client's best interest or for his own? Some planners, like Andy Hudick, argue that Schwab charges too much and that by using Schwab a planner is not putting the client's best interest first. Hudick uses Jack White and Data-Lynx (619-560-8112). But many planners will continue to use Schwab. They must disclose the conflict.

Planners say that clients often ask what kind of a deal the planner has with Schwab. Would the planner go elsewhere if it were a better deal for them, they want to know. "We tell clients that we don't get anything from Schwab except a free hookup to their computer and their SchwabLink software," says John Ueleke. Ueleke also gets a large Schwab discount. "So we tell them that they're going to have to pay somebody,"

Ueleke says. "Either we'll use Schwab, or we'll have to hire more back-office people to do things directly with the funds. That's not going to cost us as much. But it's going to cost you something." Like other planners, Bob Willard discloses the Schwab relationship and the reduced fees in his ADV.

> *"Many clients don't even see*
> *the quarterly Schwab debit.*
> *They've not written the check.*
> *Isn't that a conflict, that*
> *inertia keeps that quarterly fee*
> *coming out of the accounts?"*
>
> ANDY HUDICK

Those planners who use Schwab believe they need to keep an open mind about the relationship and to keep clients apprised of it. "When I went on the Schwab advisory board, I sent out a letter saying that being on the board doesn't mean that I wouldn't leave Schwab if somebody came up with a better idea," says Judy Shine. And James Wilson says that there are other discount brokers that offer lower fees to clients. As a fiduciary for his clients, he must continually monitor cost versus benefit and decide whether his clients are getting the best deal with Schwab.

Planners say they must also disclose to clients that there are other tradeoffs in doing business with Schwab. For example, Bob Winfield points out that Schwab customers cannot get initial public offerings, or IPOs, because Schwab does not participate in the underwriting syndicates. Likewise, customers of Schwab are not really customers of the fund companies they invest in. Sometimes that can cost them something in opportunities. For example, when PBHG in Wayne, Pennsylvania, marketed a new fund to existing shareholders in June 1996, investors who held their PBHG funds through Schwab did not get the word until the fund was closed and it was too late to get in.

Further, there are many funds that Schwab doesn't offer. Although planners disclose it to clients, it isn't typically a problem, because there are plenty of good ones to choose from. But it can be a problem when a new client comes on board with an existing portfolio.

Marilyn Capelli finds a conflict when she decides— as she typically does—to move that account to Schwab. "There are lots of funds that Schwab won't bring into the account," Capelli says. "Then I must decide: Should I continue to hold those funds outside of the account and defeat the purpose of having everything consolidated and neat? Or should I sell it to neaten things up, even though it means the client must realize capital gains?" Either way, she discloses the conflict.

Getting paid through Schwab brings up a problem, too. The advisor's fee typically comes right out of the account. One planner said Schwab mistakenly took too much from a client's account—by moving the decimal point—and the client didn't even notice. Andy Hudick believes debiting client accounts presents a major conflict. That's one of the reasons he says he doesn't use Schwab. "Many clients don't even see the quarterly Schwab debit," Hudick says. "They've not written the check. Isn't that a conflict, that inertia keeps that quarterly fee coming out of the accounts? That's the old annuity income stream for a commissioned salesperson."

To lessen that conflict, Marilyn Capelli gives clients a choice between having the fee deducted from their Schwab account or writing a check for it. "I have a few clients who send in a check," she says, "particularly those with retirement accounts." Other planners, like John Ueleke, don't debit the clients' accounts until they've mailed out an invoice. "That means we get paid in arrears," Ueleke says. "But that's what the rules say."

Finally, I've noticed many planners growing increasingly uncomfortable with what they see as the limitations and restrictions of their partnership with Schwab. In 1996, Schwab itself introduced a new conflict by announcing that it would offer financial planning services to clients. Schwab also sent faxes and mailings to clients of its financial planners, treating them as if they were Schwab customers rather than clients of a particular financial planner, or so the financial planners thought. These moves raised an alarm with planners, and a group of heavyweights traveled to Schwab's San Francisco headquarters and demanded a meeting and some reassurances.

They got them. But I still noticed some unrest at the Schwab Institutional Conference—which Schwab called Impact '96—at the Walt Disney World Dolphin in Orlando in November. I attended a dinner for some 30 top planners sponsored by the *Dow Jones Investment Advisor,* where I sat between John Bowen Jr., a planner from San Jose, California, and Bob Veres, the financial planning guru and newsletter publisher. Veres expressed his concern that the whole conference was simply too glitzy. Too much money was being spent wooing planners. For example, Veres pointed out that Schwab bought out the Epcot resort for an entire evening. Fancy vintage wines were served at breakout sessions. "I just wish Schwab had some competition," Veres told the group.

Fund companies, too, were putting on the ritz, handing out expensive trinkets in an opulent exhibit hall. One fund group had Whitey Ford signing baseballs. Don Phillips, president of Morningstar, who was sitting across the table, opined that what financial planners should be getting from Schwab and the fund companies was better deals for investors, not Whitey Ford baseballs. But John Bowen stood up to say that he was happy with the Schwab relationship. He had been one of the top planners who had confronted Schwab in the spring, and he felt pleased with Schwab's assurances.

> *"When you fully disclose*
> *everything, and you have*
> *competition that is not*
> *fully disclosing, that is the*
> *risk you have to take."*
>
> —RON ROGÉ

But I saw other signs of discontent, too. For example, I ran into Jason Zweig from *Money* magazine as he was going into the exhibit hall early one evening. Zweig, who often serves as an industry conscience, seemed disgusted by the largess. He was chronicling the freebies for a future story. It reminded me of the first financial planning conference I had attended, a lavish annual conference of the International Association for Financial Planning, held in Atlanta during the first week of October 1987, right before the stock market crash—and the subsequent fallout in the entire profession. Thousands of planners were forced out of the business in the following years, and many others struggled to regroup. I think we can expect changes in this area as the planning profession continues to evolve. Stay tuned.

5. WHAT TO SAY ABOUT RISK? Investments with higher returns carry more risk. But the return makes a better story than the risk. A planner must disclose the risk inherent in a high-return investment. "It's very important to divulge both risks and conflicts to the client," Woodhouse says. "And the fact of the matter is, people want to be sold. They don't want to look at the downside. They don't want to hear about the negatives. They want to hear about the positives."

Many of the salespeople who are your competitors are happy to comply. A salesperson might promise a 10 percent—or 20 percent—return. Guaranteed. And your job is to talk about the potential for 8 percent and to emphasize the downside risk? Forget it, you probably think.

Doing a good job as a planner inevitably means you will lose some people—the greedy and the ignorant, for sure—to salespeople who promise the moon without disclosing the risks. So be it. You cannot compete for that type of client. "When you fully disclose everything, and you have competition that is not fully disclosing, that is the risk you have to take," says Ron Rogé. "But I think it's the high road, and I think it's what you have to do."

6. HOW TO HANDLE CLIENTS IN CONFLICT?

Planners often work with couples. Many—like Cynthia Meyers—will not work with just one of the partners, because she believes that planning involves building a life together. Others—like Ross Levin—will agree to work with just one partner when the two have agreed to maintain separate assets.

All planners must decide on the rules they will follow for working with couples. And those rules are complicated for couples who decide to divorce. When two of Diahann Lassus' clients decided to divorce, both wanted to keep her as their planner. Lassus agreed. But she made a condition: If she were to keep both, they had to agree that whenever she wrote to one during the divorce process, she would send a copy to the other. Once the divorce was final, and their financial affairs were separate, they would continue as individual clients.

Judy Shine worked with three couples who divorced. All six remained clients. "But I wish I would have thought to propose Diahann's condition to them," she says. "It would have saved me a lot of grief."

Bob Winfield, who specializes in divorce, sees a lot of these problems. One of them was unique. An estate-planning lawyer referred Mr. X to Winfield for financial help with his divorce. Mr. X came in for advice and asked Winfield to take a look at a settlement plan. Then Mr. X returned with the soon-to-be ex-Mrs. X. Winfield thought that he would be asked to work out a settlement. But a couple of weeks later, the couple returned and announced their settlement to Winfield, who felt that he had been put in a box. He had been retained—theoretically—by Mr. X. But he had had no

Why Not NAPFA?

AS A REPORTER I was initially turned off by the NAPFA propaganda. I felt that NAPFA was trying to whitewash its members with the fee label—ignoring the issue of competency. And I resisted using NAPFA members. But the work I've done on this project has made me a convert. Of course, I still don't believe that you must join NAPFA to avoid conflicts of interest—or even that you must join NAPFA in order to be a top planner. Many of the best planners in the business have not joined. What these holdouts seem to have in common is an independent streak. They are professionals who choose to build their practice on their own and who resist being labeled. They are proof that you don't have to be a NAPFA member in order to become a top planner.

But if you don't join 'em, you have to beat 'em. NAPFA has—like it or not—staked out the high

hand in working out the settlement. And he worried that Mrs. X had not been represented at all.

"I felt terribly conflicted, and I basically said nothing," Winfield says. "But we talked about how they needed full disclosure of all the assets, and then I followed up with a letter to both of them and then a letter directly to her that gave her a list of competent attorneys to go to to assess the settlement, as well as the names of two additional financial advisors. So I maintained my confidence with the gentleman who had hired me to begin with, but I had also given her proper counsel by telling her that she needs to get someone to look at this from her perspective."

7. WHEN TO REFER TO THOSE WHO REFER TO YOU? For many planners, a referral network is the best source of new clients. But what do you do if

ground. The press bought the argument. That—and NAPFA's referral network—has made it much easier for NAPFA members to establish themselves.

If I were a financial planner struggling to establish myself, I would certainly be tempted to qualify for NAPFA. You can argue that membership doesn't necessarily mean you are any better. But it gives you instant credibility and the power of NAPFA's public relations machine. If you do not join, you must work very hard—as Lynn Hopewell has—to create that same kind of image for yourself.

Hopewell served as editor of the *Journal of Financial Planning* and was profiled in *Newsweek,* for example, as well as being widely quoted in the business and trade press. Those things require visibility and lots and lots of time. Establishing your reputation as an independent planner takes a lot of hard work.

another professional is a good source of new clients for you, but is not as competent in his own profession as you would like? John Ueleke gets a great deal of his business from referral sources. And he tries to make a good match between his clients and the professionals he sends them to. He wants to repay the favors. But of course his first responsibility is to his client. "If I have an attorney who feeds me a number of clients, he may or may not be the best attorney," says Ueleke. "Under what circumstances should I send a client to him? There is no question that there is a conflict there."

These conflicts are the tip of the iceberg. Even though financial planners are required to put their clients' needs first—and most are eager to do so—there are conflicts strewn throughout the relationship just as there are in any relationship between two people, like a marriage. The best you can do is to be always cognizant of the fact that the relationship serves two interests, to look for instances where there is conflict, and to consciously resolve to make the best decision for the client rather than yourself. "You're not ever going to be able to completely avoid conflicts of interest," says Myra Salzer. "Dealing with them with integrity and openness is what you must do to be effective."

WHAT'S RIGHT FOR A CLIENT?

`BEST PRACTICE` Develop a disciplined process for matching clients with the proper investments. Document in detail the information leading to your decisions.

"Investors with Heads in the Sand Fleeced by Rogue Ostrich Traders"

So goes the headline of an article in the April 1996 issue of *Financial Planning* magazine. The story goes on to say that 350 investors in 40 states shelled out about $7.45 million to invest in shares of limited partnerships organized to acquire, raise, and breed ostriches. The partnership units—which went for $7,500 to $20,000 each—were sold by two men in Thousand Palms, California, who solicited investors by cold calls and direct mailings, promising returns of 45 percent in two years, 1,147 percent in five years, 5,003 percent in eight years, and 9,355 percent in ten years. Neither of the men was registered as a broker with the Securities and Exchange Commission, according to a complaint filed by the SEC against the team.

> *"If we discover that a client has inadequate liquidity and no life or disability insurance, there may be no suitable investment for him."*
>
> — HAROLD EVENSKY

Ostrich partnerships may be one of the more outlandish schemes used to separate investors from their money. But they're as good a place as any to start a discussion on how financial advisors determine the suitability of an investment for a particular client. It is the area of suitability (or unsuitability) that generates the consumer complaints that result in most of the fantastic stories we read in the consumer press: Investors who were lured into investing their life savings in currency futures—or ostrich partnerships.

But suitability is really an ill-chosen word. It is both imprecise and easily manipulated by greedy parties on both sides of a transaction. Investors who buy into a far-fetched investment scheme, ignoring the risk while they focus on potential gains, get amnesia when the investment collapses and say it's the salesperson's fault.

On the other side of the transaction, greedy sales-people focus on how much goes into their pocket from commissions rather than what is appropriate for the client. Look at Ross Mandell, a stockbroker who had been the subject of 14 investor complaints, four job terminations for alleged misconduct, and an investigation by the New York Stock Exchange when he was profiled on the front page of *The Wall Street Journal* in the spring of 1996. Mandell, who was accused of churning clients' accounts and trading without authorization, continues to work in the securities business, the *Journal* reported. (Mandell denied the allegations.)

The National Association of Securities Dealers has set some loose suitability standards for limited partnerships—a minimum income level and net worth. But consider the example provided by Katherine Vessenes in her compliance handbook for financial planners: "One broker treated a future stream of social security payments as an asset for the sole purpose of qualifying to invest, even though the client was too young to receive them."

Stories like these prompt critics to say that the regulations for brokers and other advisors are too lax. But regulations will never remove greed from the equation. If a client agrees to take a flier, nothing prevents him from later complaining that he was tricked by the broker. If the broker is focused on himself rather than the client, he will find a way to get the money into his pocket. "This is not fun and games," Mandell told his fellow stockbrokers, according to the *Journal* report. "You can have fun when you work, but for me, this is the pursuit of cash. I want to be wealthy."

Beyond "Know Your Client"

THERE ARE SOME REGULATIONS in place for those who recommend securities. Brokers are registered representatives who work for a broker/dealer. "Registered" means that they are licensed by the Securities and Exchange Commission and the New York Stock Exchange. These registered reps are governed by the "know your client" rules, which require them to determine at the time of sale whether a product is a suitable investment for a particular customer.

Technically, financial planners are held to a higher standard than the know-your-client rules because they are fiduciaries. While a broker is required to determine suitability at the time of sale, a fiduciary must look at the client's entire financial situation and determine first whether he should be investing at all. These duties are outlined in the certified financial planner code of ethics. "If you're a CFP, you have to sign off on that," Ross Levin says.

Beyond that, the legal requirements for "suitability" are minimal. Many planners are not regulated by the National Association of Securities Dealers because they do not hold securities licenses. Financial planners who give investment advice are required to register as investment advisors under the Investment Advisers Act of 1940. Under this act, there is no similar "know your customer" standard. "The only requirement for a registered investment advisor is disclosure," says Harold Evensky. An advisor who registers under the 1940 act must provide clients with Form ADV, Part II, which describes the advisor's background and business relationships.

In May 1994, the SEC proposed rules on the suitability of investment advice provided by investment advisors. In the proposed regulation, the SEC says that financial advisors are fiduciaries who owe their clients a series of duties, including full disclosure of conflicts of interest, "utmost and exclusive loyalty," the duty of best execution on trades, and "the duty to provide only suitable investment advice."

The proposed rules would require an advisor to inquire into the client's financial situation, investment experience, and investment objective before making any investment recommendations. In other words, an advisor would have to know about a client's cash flow, income, retirement needs, insurance situation, and so forth before making investment recommendations.

But two years later, in mid 1996, the SEC had taken no action on the rules, according to John Heine, an SEC spokesman, who said, "it is not scheduled for action any time soon."

Most financial planners are not eager for more federal and state regulation. But top advisors are already doing just what these regulations propose. "It's very basic," says Eleanor Blayney. "You make the best choice for the client rather than the best choice for yourself. The standard is: What would you advise your mother to do if she were sitting across the table, instead of the client?" And, of course, the best planners do probe into the client's financial situation, just as the SEC proposed, to make certain that all financial needs are being met. Sometimes the search for suitable investments ends there. "If we discover that a client has inadequate liquidity and no life or disability insurance, there may be no suitable investment for him," Evensky says.

But most clients do become investors. Here the planner's job is to use investments that will help the client meet his goals and, perhaps more importantly, to convince the client to stick with the investments. Planners begin to explore their client's needs at the initial meeting. "This is very conversational," says Marilyn Capelli. "I want to learn how they view their situation and what they are looking for." At this meeting, Capelli takes lots of notes but doesn't ask for statistics. She's looking more at issues of style. Most planners are straightforward about their own style, too. They talk about how they work, how they invest, what the client can expect from them, and where they will draw the line. Then they ask the client to bring in a number of documents, including information on:

◆ income
◆ estimated budget
◆ existing investments
◆ assets and liabilities
◆ marital status
◆ insurance coverage
◆ financial goals
◆ family obligations, age, health and mortality issues
◆ two years' tax returns
◆ company benefit booklets
◆ loan agreements
◆ will and trust documents
◆ stock-option agreements
◆ investment account statements

Planners want to see the documents firsthand rather than taking a client's word for what he has. Consider what happened to David M. Bradt Jr., a partner at Arthur Andersen LLP in Tyson's Corner, Virginia. One of his clients told Bradt that he had set up a combination money-purchase/profit-sharing retirement plan in 1986 and that he was contributing 20 percent a year to it. When the balance grew to more than $100,000, requiring Bradt to file a Form 5500, he asked his client to bring in the documentation. "It turned out that he had only checked the box for a profit-sharing plan," Bradt recalls. "So he had over-funded the plan for seven years." Bradt had to file amended tax returns for each of the years. "What we didn't really prepare him for was the blizzard of paper," Bradt said. "Every piece of mail he got from the IRS was in septuplet. For each year, he got the same notice seven times."

Once the material is gathered, the first step in investing is to set goals. Second is to determine the rate of investment return necessary to accomplish those goals. And third is to figure out what level of risk is inherent in those returns. The planner might find that the client needs to take very little risk to meet his goals.

"If we assess everything they own and find they've actually met their objectives, I say, 'Wait a minute. Why should we take any risk at all with this client?'" says Katharine McGee. From the goal-setting exercise, a planner develops an investment-policy statement including the target rate of return and standard deviations. McGee shows the target rate of return and one to two standard deviations so a client can get a feel for the range of possible results. (One standard deviation encompasses two-thirds of the expected returns. Two standard deviations include 95 percent of expected returns.)

> *"When a client says, 'I want to hit the ball out of the park,' you educate them out of that idea, or you say, 'That's not what we do.'"*
>
> —ELEANOR BLAYNEY

Risk Tolerance

TOP PLANNERS WORK WITH A small core of investments, chiefly mutual funds, that they put together in portfolios depending on the client's needs and risk tolerance. But most planners feel a duty to go beyond assessing a client's risk comfort level and then matching it up to a suitable investment. That strategy might well leave the client short of his financial goals. Instead, they must assess the client's resources and goals and then write a prescription to help the client achieve his goals. If the client protests that investing in stocks is too risky, he won't get away with it unless he has plenty of money to meet his goals. "You may do something that is suitable for someone's risk tolerance, but if they invest in that manner they will never meet their quality-of-life standards," says Harold Evensky.

Evensky, who specializes in investing, says he finds it puzzling that some planners let clients decide how much risk they're going to take. "When I go to a physician, and he says: 'You've got to have surgery,' and I refuse, maybe he'll tell me the next-best thing I can do," Evensky says. "I'll certainly do that for a client. I won't force them to do something they don't want to do. But why should I let them decide what they'll invest in? That's what they're paying me for. I have to educate them to accept my advice." Likewise, he doesn't spend much time figuring out a client's "money personality." "Some people are afraid of needles, but doctors don't treat them differently because of their 'medical personality,'" Evensky says. "People have needs, there are risks in getting there, and our job is to help educate and develop the comfort level as much as we can."

Still, Evensky does acknowledge that risk tolerance can determine staying power. If a client cannot tolerate volatility, he might bail out at just the wrong time, which turns a suitable portfolio into an unsuitable one. That makes the client's staying power one of the key aspects to determining suitability. Ross Levin points out that risk is not just about volatility. A good planner looks at all types of risk to a client's financial well-being. Still, planners are aware that it is volatility—not inflation—that sends investors running for the exits. "You and I will agree that volatility is not the ultimate risk that threatens financial well-being," says Eleanor Blayney. "Volatility goes away. But we're dealing with clients who perceive risk as volatility. The real key to investment success is staying power. Are they going to stay with it?"

This is one of the key lessons I learned while doing the research for this book. In the consumer writing I have done, I've always dismissed the notion of risk tolerance as a lot of noise. Put your money in stocks and hold your nose was my best advice to readers. But I was wrong. I discovered—both by talking to planners and by talking to friends and acquaintances about their investing experiences—the fear that one dollar could ever be less than a dollar is very real for many people. If they lose money, they're gone. It's as simple as that.

That hit home when I was talking to a friend who is the chief investment officer of a big money-management firm. She confided that she and her husband, a Ph.D. arts consultant, had missed the bull market of the past decade because they had all their money in cash. Her husband simply could not bring himself to invest in stocks. Several years earlier, her firm had assigned her a financial planner as an executive perk. The planner had finally persuaded her husband to start moving into the stock market at the beginning of 1996, dollar cost averaging beginning in January. Clearly, the planner did not know anything more about investments than my friend did. But he did her an invaluable service. "It took him four years to do it," my friend said. "But it was worth it." I now believe that this might be the most important of the investment services that planners provide.

This is a favorite topic of Eleanor Blayney, who's given a great deal of thought to the subject of suitability and risk tests. "Assessing risk tolerance is really assessing the client's staying power in your investment program," Blayney told a group of planners at the 1995 Conference for Advanced Planning in Washington, D.C. "The planner's job is to make the ride as comfortable as possible." To Blayney, determining suitability means you must use some type of risk tolerance instrument, even though none of them do a particularly good job.

"I divide risk questionnaires into two camps," Blayney says. "I find each of them deficient." The first is what she calls the "Roger Gibson type of thing," referring to the Pittsburgh money manager and former planner who wrote the bible on asset allocation. In this exercise, clients are given ten portfolios with differing amounts of equities. Each has expected rates of return and ranges of returns. The client is asked to run his finger down the portfolios and tell the planner where he starts getting nervous. "So you see that he stops at a portfolio with 70 percent equities and the possibility of a negative 10 percent," Blayney says. "The client points to the negative 10 percent and says: 'That's it. That's all I can take.'"

"If we assess everything they own and find they've actually met their objectives, I say, 'Wait a minute. Why should we take any risk at all with this client?'"

— KATHARINE McGEE

The good news is that this questionnaire is "instantly mappable into a portfolio," Blayney says. The bad news is that most clients haven't really processed the information. They have not seriously considered how they will feel if their $10,000 is suddenly worth just $9,000. Should a bad year come along, and the portfolio take a 10 percent hit, the client is likely to be gone. So the planner hasn't really learned anything.

The second type is the "personality test," à la planner and money psychologist Kathleen Gurney, author of "Your Money Personality: What It Is and How You Can Profit From It." Gurney focuses on money quirks and dysfunctional money personalities. "These tests may tell you a whole lot about the client," Blayney says. "You may know them better than their mother does by the time you finish with this thing. But it doesn't necessarily tell you anything about their investment behavior. There are people who love to hang-glide but will not invest in anything but CDs." So, Blayney says, "you have questionnaires that can go instantly into a portfolio but totally miss the point—the human element or the fear or the greed. Or you've got personality tests that tell you a great deal about the client but don't give you many investment guidelines."

Still, Blayney, who is a member of the ethics committee of the International Association for Financial Planning, says planners are obligated to do something to determine risk tolerance. And they must prove that they've gone to the trouble. She found that 90 percent of the cases under review by the ethics committee involved suitability issues. "In every single case, no risk tolerance instrument was ever used," she says. "That probably contributed to the dispute in the first place, and it may also determine who wins a subsequent lawsuit."

Blayney suggests that planners first test themselves. Think about how you describe an investment program, she says. Do you use a richer vocabulary to describe the upside than the downside? Blayney says it is difficult, even for her, to fathom how a client will react to the daily ups and downs of the market, because she has become so desensitized to them herself. So she likes to compare being new to the market to the way she feels when she looks under the hood of her car, and a mechanic tells her, "Lady, you need a new distributor cap." She doesn't even know what that is.

Blayney offers some basic guidelines for looking at risk. For instance, you should use an instrument that includes enough questions for you to be able to detect inconsistencies. Often clients won't understand some of the questions the way they're phrased or may use words in different ways than you do. Blayney also suggests that the assessment process be educational, allowing clients to learn more about the alternatives rather than forcing them to make decisions from limited knowledge.

She also suggests that you learn as much as you can about investor psychology. For instance, she has found that many investors care more about how many investments lose money than about the total lost. So if a client loses $100 in investment A, $100 in investment B, and $150 in investment C, he is likely to be more panicky than if he loses $350 in one investment and the others increase in value. Knowing that can help you tailor the way you do your quarterly investment reports and the way you deal with clients. For instance, in a good quarter, Blayney might say: Investment A was up, Investment B was up, and Investment C was up. In a bad quarter, she might say: The entire portfolio was down, and here's why. Of course, Blayney also looks at each report before it goes out and flags those clients that she will call personally as soon as they receive them.

Evensky uses a risk quiz that he developed himself chiefly to get clients to acknowledge that they can't have it both ways. "We ask the same question a lot of different ways," he says: "How long can you put this money away? When will you need the money? And so forth." He also uses a matrix with numbers one through six and asks clients to circle a number for each question, with one being of little import and six being very important. The first question asks about the importance of capital preservation. "Everyone circles six, and then they think they're finished," Evensky says. But number two asks about the importance of inflation protection. "It's sort of 'I gotcha,'" Evensky says. "They know they can't put it in T-bills and have inflation protection, too." Evensky's quiz is reproduced in his book, "Wealth Management."

Most planners have developed their own series of questions to get a feel for a client's investment experiences. Blayney asks clients how they were invested at the beginning of October 1987 and where they were at the end of the month. Jane King researches the investments she recommends to see how they fared in the 1987 crash and asks clients: "If that happened tomorrow, how would you feel?" Bob Willard asks clients for the best and worst investments they've made, as well as some they've walked away from.

Ross Levin likes to point out the other side of risk: He explains to clients that a diversified portfolio reduces risks, but it can also reduce the upside. For example, his clients' diversified portfolios returned about 20 percent in 1995 when the U.S. market, as measured by the Standard & Poor's 500 stock index, soared over 37 percent. "So you have to work on the other side of staying power, too," Levin says. He also gives clients a forced-choice decision. He lists the characteristics that you might want your investments to have. Then he gives clients nine points to spread among four categories, which are:

1. Produce income
2. Maintain principal
3. Grow faster than inflation
4. Provide tax advantages

"If you give them just nine points to spread among those four categories, they begin to put a value on what they want," Levin says in his book, "Wealth Management Index." "The client also begins to realize that there is a relative value among choices. No individual investment does all things."

David Drucker says he helps clients explore concepts like time, volatility, credit quality, and so forth. Then he tries to move them gradually up the risk ladder a step or two at a time. Like other top planners, he takes notes on all of the conversations he has with clients and files documentation on how he determined risk tolerance, including questionnaires or quizzes.

Managing Their Expectations

PERSUADING CLIENTS TO TAKE ON some risk is one challenge. Toning down overly ambitious expectations is another. In early 1996, Eleanor Blayney met with a prospective client who made this demand: "I want 4 or 5 percent above the S&P in a bull market, and I want a guaranteed return of 5 percent in down markets." Blayney told him he would have to choose: "Which is more important?" she asked him. "You can't have both." Blayney admits it's sometimes tough to be so candid. "We are all struggling entrepreneurs, and we can overpromise or overcommit and not be able to deliver," Blayney says. "Managing expectations is defining who you are as a planner, what you accept, and what you will do." In this case, Blayney says that what you know is less important than what you believe. "There has to be that exchange of what your core beliefs and values are," she said. "It's like that horrible bumper sticker: 'He who dies with the most toys wins.' You have to be clear that that's not how you see the game."

Instead, Blayney says, you must explain to clients what you believe is possible in terms of investment performance, what your role is going to be, and what you're going to do. "When a client says, 'I want to hit the ball out of the park,' you educate them out of that idea, or you say, 'That's not what we do,'" Blayney says. "We tell people that we believe the best results are achieved with discipline and patience." If you can't manage expectations, do you turn clients away? "We do it very reluctantly and with far too much difficulty," Blayney says. "When we do, it comes from the sense that we will not work well together, from values that are not congruent."

Often it's the client who proposes an unsuitable investment. What to do when a client asks you to buy something that you consider a bad move? Most planners just say no. For example, one afternoon, Linda Lubitz met with a doctor and his wife who were new clients. The doctor had a million dollars in his pension plan, and his wife held all the money outside the plan in her name. Lubitz had developed an asset-allocation model and an investment-policy statement that the clients had signed off on. Then the doctor told her that he'd met a young man at a spa in Mexico who had

> *"Clients send me private placement stuff all the time. I think they just want me to talk them out of it."*
>
> — ROSS LEVIN

a brand new company with a wonderful product. The doctor wanted to invest $10,000. "Where are you going to get the money, Bernie?" Lubitz asked him. "From my pension plan," he replied. Lubitz told him that pension accounts should never be used for speculative investments. "If you lose the money, two bad things will happen to you," Lubitz said. "First, you can't take the loss against gains. Second, you can't ever replace that money in a tax-deferred environment." The doctor looked at his wife: "So can we buy the stock from your money?" he asked. "No," she said. And that was that.

Other planners are willing to compromise. Elaine Bedel offers her opinion on the investment, but says she would ultimately buy it if the client insisted. "I think it's my responsibility to educate them and give them an honest opinion," Bedel says. "But if they still insist, I'd probably go ahead and do it, making it clear that they are responsible for that investment." For Ross Levin, the frequency of the requests is the key. "Clients send me private placement stuff all the time," Levin says. "I think they just want me to talk them out of it." But if Levin sees a pattern developing—the same client coming over and over with "hot tips"—he often decides that he and the client don't see eye to eye and suggests they part ways. "If I'm constantly showered with this stuff, I know I won't satisfy them," he says. "So sometimes it means that I don't work with a particular client."

What's In, What's Out

ALL OF THESE PLANNERS WORK from a menu of investments they have developed for clients. "There is no such thing as a bad investment, short of fraud," Evensky says. "There are inappropriate investments. But almost any investment might be appropriate for some client in an appropriate percentage." Still, Evensky, like most good planners, eliminates a lot of investments for clients that he might well use for himself *(see Chapter 7, "Providing Due Diligence," page 164)*. "There are a lot of things that we simply don't consider because our evaluation of our client psychology is that they say they can live with something, but if it goes bad, we know they won't live with it," he says. For example, Evensky doesn't use junk bonds. "It's not that we think they're inappropriate or unsuitable," he says. "But we think people won't sleep well when the market turns against them."

Most planners say they use only marketable securities. Most don't use limited partnerships, options, commodities, or short sales. (Bob Willard, who specializes in real estate and limited partnerships, is an exception. He believes his expertise in these areas has given him a special niche.) Most won't buy gold, real estate, or energy directly, either. "I will buy Jean Marie Eveillard's SoGen International to get some gold in the portfolio," McGee says. "That's one of the reasons I like that particular fund. Or we may use Vanguard's energy fund if the client is concerned about investment hedges. But we won't buy energy directly."

When professionals design portfolios, they talk about the efficient frontier. In his investment classic, "Asset Allocation," money manager Roger Gibson says that "a portfolio that minimizes portfolio risk for a given expected return (or equivalently maximizes portfolio expected return for a given level of risk) is said to be efficient. If we join together all the efficient portfolios for a given set of investment alternatives, we form what is called the efficient frontier."

The objective, Gibson says, is to allocate assets in such a way as to create a portfolio that lies on the efficient frontier. "These portfolios have less risk than any other portfolio with equivalent expected return, or alternatively, have more return than any other portfolio with equivalent risk." Once a portfolio is on the efficient frontier, the only way to increase the return of that portfolio is to take on more risk.

Blayney thinks of her clients as having two different profiles on the efficient frontier. With the first type, she simply wants to reduce risk, "sort of bringing them up to the frontier where they can get the same or better return for less risk." The second set "is actually on the frontier, and what you're really doing is adding more and more risk for more return." Blayney says: "It's very critical to decide which kind of client you're working with."

Evensky, a friend of Gibson, has designed 12 model portfolios for clients to achieve real rates of return, after inflation, that range from 3.5 percent to 7 percent. "We start at 50/50 stocks and bonds as a baseline," Evensky says. "That's a 4 percent real rate of return." But he also has two fixed-income portfolios designed for returns of 3.5 and 3.85 percent. Two portfolios are designed for maximum growth. And one portfolio is

They Made the Cut

TOP FINANCIAL ADVISORS work from a list of investments that they have researched for client portfolios. They look for consistent performance, low expenses, and investment style. Of course, not all investments go into each client's portfolio. But most clients will end up with a portfolio that is derived from this list.

Here is a list of the mutual funds used by Marilyn Capelli. Capelli points out that not all clients start with a blank slate. Many clients come to her with a group of investments. She may not want to sell all of them because she doesn't want to take the capital gains. In that case, she works around what the client has, adding additional investments from her list to round out the portfolio.

Specialty Classes
Real Estate: Cohen & Steers Realty
Energy: Vanguard Special Energy
Utilities: Strong American Utilities

Balanced
Dodge & Cox Balanced
Rainier Balanced
Lindner Dividend
Berwyn Income

Bond Funds
Municipal Bond: Vanguard Municipal Bond funds for very short to intermediate term
Strong Municipal Bond
Price Tax-Free High Yield

Taxable Bonds
Stein Roe Income
Northeast Investors (High Yield)
American Century Benham GNMA

Strong Advantage
PIMCO Total Return
(Capelli also uses individual treasuries, corporates,
and municipal bonds in most portfolios)

Large Companies
Neuberger & Berman (Value)
Mutual Shares (Value)
Price Dividend (Growth)
Harbor Capital Appreciation (Growth)
Vanguard Index 500

Mid-Cap Companies
Oakmark (Value)
Mutual Beacon (Value)
Strong Opportunity
Rainier Core Equities
Robertson Stephens Val+Gro (Growth)
PBHG Growth (Growth)

Small Companies
Mutual Discovery (Value—also foreign)
Royce Premier (Value)
Wasatch Growth
Baron Asset (Growth)
Columbia Special (Growth)
Heartland Value
Price Small Cap Value

Foreign/International
Price International Stock
SoGen International
Managers International Equity
Montgomery Institutional Emerging Markets
Harbor International

100 percent equities, which is designed for 7 percent real return. His maximum international allocations are 18 percent to developed countries and 16 percent to emerging markets. "Intellectually, I'm comfortable going higher," Evensky says. "But clients aren't comfortable going higher. As the clients get more sophisticated, I will relax the constraints on emerging markets." Every six months he reviews all his assumptions and allocations. "But our goal is to not change allocations more than every three or four years," he says.

If only investors were able to leave their emotions out of the equation, finding suitable investments would be pure science. You would simply design the portfolio that would get the best potential return over the time period the client had available, and that would be that.

It is your clients' feelings about volatility—and their tendency to bolt when the going gets rough—that makes designing a portfolio an art. This was brought home to me in the fall of 1996. I had just finished writing this book when I left to travel across the country on a book tour for an earlier book, "A Commonsense Guide to Mutual Funds." So the problems faced by financial planners were fresh in my mind when I began doing investment seminars for consumers in late September.

At the time, the Dow Jones Industrial Average was teasing the 6,000 mark. As I traveled, it broke through 6,000. Of course, the newspapers were full of it. Where would the market go next? 7,000? 5,000? What I saw in the investors who attended the bookstore seminars I gave was incredible anxiety. Was it too late to get in the market? they wanted to know. Was it time to get out? What was the best course of action? I told them all the same thing: that I didn't believe in timing the market; that it was the biggest single mistake most investors made. Still, at every single seminar, someone came up afterward and asked me privately: "But what do you really think the market is going to do now?"

PROVIDING DUE DILIGENCE

BEST PRACTICE Choose the asset class-

es you will use and find the most consistent,

lowest-cost money managers in each one.

Document your decisions and the process

you use.

Financial planners are required to

research investments before they select

them for a client portfolio—to do their due

diligence to make certain that their choice

is a sound one. Naturally, that includes

reading the offering prospectus, the mar-

keting materials, and any objective analysis

that is available. It includes checking the

expenses, the manager's philosophy, the

investment style, and so forth. It might also

include talking to the money manager and looking at portfolio investments. If an investment blows up, an advisor who has not completed and documented the method he used to complete his due diligence could be in trouble.

Consider then what happened to Manager's Intermediate Mortgage Fund, a bond fund that was popular with financial planners until it hit the skids when interest rates spiked in the spring of 1994. Even those planners who had done their homework were caught off guard, because the fund had much more of its assets invested in volatile derivatives than was evident in the fund's literature or in talks with the manager. "It was much more vulnerable to changes in interest rates than research led us to believe," says Harold Evensky. "The quoted duration was not meaningful in terms of its market exposure."

As the fund headed south, planners began heading for the exits. Evensky watched as other planners pulled client money out of the fund when it dropped 12 and 15 percent, largely because he believes in sticking with the investments he selects. But eventually he decided he wasn't getting the full story from the manager. If the manager wasn't doing what he said he was doing, then Evensky figured all bets were off. "We bailed out, and it still continued to go down," Evensky says. He says the experience left his firm more wary of derivatives. "We learned something," he says. "We don't entirely avoid them, but we tread very lightly in anything with derivatives in it since then."

When we talked about due diligence on a conference call during the research for this book, Stan Hargrave, a planner who specializes in representing financial planners and registered reps who have been sued by clients for making investment choices that turned out poorly, pointed to Manager's Intermediate as an example of how too much due diligence can be a mistake. Those planners who assured their clients that they went beyond the surface to do something extra in due diligence assumed extra liability for that fund's problems.

Here is Hargrave's argument: Let's say you took your due diligence seriously. You told your clients that you talked to the manager periodically just to touch base and make certain everything was going as planned. When it turned out that the manager was deviating from what the investment objectives outlined in the prospectus permitted him to do, your liability would be greater.

> *"If you didn't realize that the funds you were using had that exposure, and you didn't realize they could fall apart, that's a big liability."*
>
> — LOU STANASOLOVICH

"You can get yourself into trouble and raise the drawbridge as a reward for doing more extensive due diligence," he explains. "So if I were a good attorney, and you were telling me about all this wonderful due diligence that you did on Manager's Intermediate Mortgage, you just opened Pandora's box. Then I would really start digging into your mode of investigation and how you did it and why you didn't uncover the fact that the manager violated the investment objectives of the fund, if you did such great due diligence."

On the other hand, an advisor who acknowledged that his due diligence consisted of reading the Morningstar report, the prospectus, and the semiannual report might fare better in a lawsuit. This advisor could legitimately say that he got no clue from these documents that the fund's manager was violating his mandate, Hargrave says.

Does that mean planners should do minimum due diligence? Many planners would say yes. But the top planners do not choose to squeeze under the fence like an escaping Peter Rabbit. "That reminds me of my physician clients who are worried from morning until evening that someone will sue them," says Ram Kolluri. Instead, they do the very best due diligence they can do. And then they accept the consequences. That, like accepting the label of fiduciary, is part of being a good planner.

"If you, in good faith, do your very best, and your very best isn't good enough, and someone sues you, then so be it," Kolluri says. He documents all of his research. And then he accepts what comes.

Harold Evensky, an expert in this area who frequently conducts continuing-education workshops for planners on due diligence, fully accepted the responsibility for Manager's Intermediate. "We should be responsible," he said. "We were responsible. And we should have picked up on that kind of exposure. We are prepared to accept the consequences because we do believe we're going beyond the minimum of what we must do. We learned a lesson here."

Of course, failing to do in-depth due diligence doesn't provide an escape hatch either. It's something of a Catch-22. After doing the research for this book, I've concluded that you should do the most in-depth due diligence you can. "It's much worse if you don't do the due diligence," says Lou Stanasolovich, pointing to the debacle in emerging-market bonds in December 1994. Lots of domestic equity funds—like Fidelity Asset Manager—held these bonds, although you wouldn't have found that out by reading the prospectus. If one of your clients lost money in Asset Manager, would you feel comfortable assuring him that you'd read the prospectus and hadn't picked up the potential problem? "If you didn't realize that the funds you were using had that exposure, and you didn't realize they could fall apart, that's a big liability," Stanasolovich says. Much of this information can be gleaned by talking to the manager directly, which most top planners do either individually or on conference calls.

So if you want to join the ranks of the elite, you must determine to do the most complete research possible before putting client money in an investment. Unfortunately, there is no road map here. "The law of compliance is one of reasonableness and conventional practice," says Tim Kochis, who is a lawyer as well as a planner. "But right now, there is very little conventional practice about the appropriate investigation of mutual funds. So we're all hanging out there. Whatever we do, it could easily be determined that it is not enough just because there is very little to go on."

What will eventually happen, Kochis says, is that standards will emerge out of what the best people in the industry are doing in due diligence. And that's what we're going to tell you about. You might as well be in the vanguard rather than bringing up the rear.

The Straight and Narrow

DUE DILIGENCE MAY NOT BE formalized. But it has come a long way in a short time. A decade ago, financial planners eagerly sold a mutual fund based chiefly on the fund's marketing literature and performance records. Today, advisors who use mutual funds in client portfolios start with their own list of asset categories. Then they look to see which managers use those categories and whether they are pure and consistent. By demanding style consistency, financial advisors and other institutional investors are revolutionizing the mutual-fund business, helping to assure the success of consistent, low-cost performers like the Vanguard Group, Dimensional Fund Advisors, and

PIMCO, and working as an agent of change in offerings of groups like Fidelity Investments.

Fidelity has traditionally given totally free rein to fund managers to invest wherever they choose. Financial advisors who see it as their job to decide where their money will be invested shun the lone rangers at Fidelity. And Fidelity responded in the spring of 1996 by shuffling 26 portfolio managers, promising that its funds would be more consistent and that it would impose more control from the top.

> *"We tell our clients that asset allocation is the most important and that within any asset class, we try to find the single manager who we think is going to ride that horse best."*

—TIM KOCHIS

All of these changes are recent ones, fostered by a small core of elite planners who continue to hone their mutual-fund selection process. "Sometimes we forget that up until five years ago, when a mutual fund called itself a small-cap fund, we just took them at their word and put in the money," says Stanasolovich. "Over those short five years, all of the investigations that we do today have developed." Stanasolovich believes that due diligence has quadrupled during those five years and that it will quadruple again by the year 2000, as planners continue to look for ways to evaluate the investments they use.

Top planners see themselves as managers of a client portfolio. Most use mutual funds because that is the most efficient way to get broad diversification. But the planner sees asset allocation as the most important investment decision he will make for clients. That means choosing the asset classes—and funds to represent them—and then using just a handful of funds. Lou Stanasolovich has just 40 funds on his recommended list. And he doesn't add them to the list until he visits the manager. Tim Kochis uses just ten, in different allocations, for each client. "We tell our clients that asset allocation is the most important and that within any asset class, we try to find the single manager who we think is going to ride that horse best," Kochis says. "When that horse is no longer the best horse to bet on, we fire that horse and find another one."

Kochis starts with an index fund—the Schwab 1000 or the Vanguard 500—for large-cap stocks. "We believe that the large-cap domestic end of the market is really quite efficient," Kochis says. "So we use indexes." For the small cap and international pieces of the portfolio, he uses active managers. But not too many. "Rather than becoming closet indexers by having a multiplicity of funds that are balancing out manager performance, we are trying very hard to find the very best managers and making big bets on them," he says. Ram Kolluri, too, says he continues to move to index funds because they offer purity and low expenses. "I've backed myself more and more into index funds, so that today, it's a substantial portion of my portfolio," he says.

Index funds offer clear advantages to planners in doing due diligence. But they don't eliminate the need for it. There can be huge differences in expenses, in performance, and in the indexes that the funds use as a benchmark. Lou Stanasolovich completed a study in 1995 that looked at all the index funds in the Morningstar universe. "The return pattern was generally the same, but the performance difference was really significant," he says. "I was just shocked." On the domestic funds, there was as much as 70 basis points' difference in performance, Stanasolovich says. On those that track Morgan Stanley's Europe, Asia, and Far East Index, or EAFE, there was as much as 200 basis points' difference.

Consider the single-country indexes that debuted in mid 1996 as an example. Morgan Stanley & Co. introduced funds that invested in 17 different countries, which it called World Equity Benchmark Shares (or WEBS), and Deutsche Morgan Grenfell introduced nine single-country funds, which it called Country Baskets. Kolluri, who had spent two years developing a model to determine which international markets are mispriced, was excited about the opportunity to capitalize on it by using these new products. Like closed-end funds, these indexes start with a fixed number of shares and trade on major stock exchanges. But they are designed to resolve the major problem of closed-end funds, which is that many of them trade at a premium or a discount to net asset value.

To do that, the WEBS and Country Baskets incorporate a feature of open-end funds, designed to provide market hedgers with an opportunity to trade them in bulk. Like an open-end fund, these funds create and redeem shares as needed, though only in large aggregations ($2 million to $5 million) and on an in-kind basis. For example, an investor who wants 100,000 shares of Morgan Stanley's Australia Fund must deliver an equivalent selection of Australian stocks that make up that fund.

So far, so good. And so complex. But the indexes presented an additional problem for Kolluri. Both were index funds, true. But they used different indexes. Deutsche Morgan Grenfell's Country Baskets replicate the *Financial Times*/Standard & Poor's actuaries' world indexes in each of nine countries. And

Morgan Stanley & Co.'s 17 World Equity Benchmark Shares—WEBS—are based on a statistical sampling of stocks in the 17 countries represented by WEBS. The teams of investment bankers who designed these complex instruments offered arguments for why their product was the only way to proceed. For their part, the people at Deutsche said that only by replicating an index could one get a true investment in that country. Their funds bought every single stock in the countries they invested in, making an index that was guaranteed to replicate a pure play in that country. But Morgan responded that buying all the stocks in an index overexposed the investor to illiquid markets. Some of the stocks could not be readily bought and sold. That would make the Country Baskets too expensive, Morgan said, and too illiquid. So sampling was better. That left Kolluri to do his due diligence on which was the better way to index.

No Substitute for Thinking

HOW TO DO THE BEST POSSIBLE job of selecting mutual-fund investments for your clients? We turned to Harold Evensky, a financial advisor who makes frequent presentations on the topic. Start by thinking through your own investment philosophy, reading the academic research, and thinking about how you will put a portfolio together, Evensky suggests. You want to be in control of the process. Investing requires discipline and a plan. That is your job. Don't defer to the marketing department of the fund companies to sell you on their funds. Decide what you want and go after it.

The research is a starting point. But you must figure out how to implement it by using mutual funds. If that were a piece of cake, your clients wouldn't need you. For example, research shows that the stock market offers the best return. You can add 5 percentage points to a T-bill return by investing in stocks. No surprise here. "We all know that the market gets 5 percent over

T-bills," Evensky says. Research shows that small company stocks can add another 5 percent. And that value investing adds 5 percent more. If you heed that research, should you put all your client's money in small-cap value funds? No. This is where you earn your fee. Evensky buys the research. But he doesn't buy the funds.

Although value investing wins out over growth, most value mutual funds do not do a good job of delivering value. John Rekenthaler, publisher of *Morningstar Mutual Funds,* wrote an article on this topic in the April 1995 issue of *Morningstar Investor.* Rekenthaler's research showed that value investing dominates the academic studies, but not the performance charts. Rekenthaler found that actively managed funds, in general, lagged the indexes by an amount that can be explained by trading costs and other fees. But when the funds are broken down by type, growth managers generally did better than the index. But value managers lagged by a mile. That's chiefly because growth stock winners are easier to identify.

"A good value manager doesn't own stocks," Evensky says. "He owns a kennel of dogs. No one wants to admit to owning these things. But it's the dead dogs that don't die that make the money." Thanks to this research, Evensky has decided that he will use active managers for growth stocks and passive managers for value. Those are the kinds of decisions that you must make for your clients.

Knowing what you want is one thing. Finding it is another. You must do that by opening up the hood and looking inside a fund. You won't make much headway by looking at the fund's objectives. "The stated objectives are absolutely worthless," Evensky says. "But that's what your clients are most familiar with, so you have to understand [the objectives]." You should be familiar with the labels used in the industry, such as balanced equity income and aggressive growth, simply for your own education. But you should not use the labels to set up your asset classes or to make investment decisions.

Consider Fidelity Balanced Fund. "It sounds pretty conservative," Evensky says, "kind of a sleep-tight fund that invests in stocks and bonds." But in mid 1995, half of the portfolio was in foreign stocks. Fidelity Blue Chip, another soothing name, had 25 percent of its assets overseas and 11 percent in small-cap stocks. "The important thing is, we need to know these terms," Evensky says. "We need to know what they supposedly mean, and we need to be able to explain to clients why we are not using those classifications." This is an important step in managing client expectations, he says.

> *"I've backed myself more and*
> *more into index funds, so*
> *that today, it's a substantial*
> *portion of my portfolio."*

— RAM KOLLURI

Rather than buying into the labels fund companies use, do your own investigative work. "Fundamental analysis is the most important," Evensky says. That includes the work you do yourself as well as whatever you can find that has been done by objective observers like Ibbotson, Value Line, and Morningstar. For example, Evensky likes Morningstar's fundamental factor analysis that results in the nine-square Morningstar style box. "They look at a few statistics like the price-to-earnings ratio, and they say a fund falls into one of nine boxes," Evensky says. They are large-cap growth, value, and blend; mid-cap growth, value, and blend;

and small-cap growth, value, and blend. Unlike the stated objective, which is meaningless, the style box does say something about the way a fund operates. Morningstar also provides a style-box history so that you can look back and see how consistent a manager has been.

Evensky also likes style analysis, the approach used by Nobel laureate William Sharpe to regress a portfolio's returns against a benchmark to see how well it matches. The approach is controversial. Don Phillips, president of Morningstar, argues that this statistical factor analysis does not tell you what is in the portfolio, only how a portfolio behaves, and that it is therefore not very useful. In other words, it might act like a portfolio that is 40 percent in long-term bonds. But it might hold no long-term bonds at all.

Evensky dismisses that. "This is the 'it walks like a duck, quacks like a duck, so it's a duck' approach," Evensky says. If the portfolio behaves as if it were 40 percent in long-term bonds, that's a useful piece of information for Evensky. "Style analysis can be very helpful," he says. "It should not be the be-all and end-all. But you need to incorporate it." For style analysis, Evensky consults William Sharpe on the Internet *(see "Resources," page 301)*. He uses an analysis product from Wilson Associates Int'l. (818-999-0015), HYSALES from CDA/Weisenberger (800-232-2285), and Morningstar. But what he likes best is Ibbotson's Style Analyzer (312-616-1620). "Every advisor needs to make a philosophical decision about style," Evensky says. "At a minimum, you need to separate your managers in terms of style."

As an investment advisor, you must think about whether you will use active managers or passive managers, too. Active managers believe that even after commissions, trading costs, and other fees, they can beat the system. "Passive managers believe that they're lying or crazy," Evensky says. "A passive manager doesn't necessarily believe the market is perfectly efficient. But he believes it's so efficient that after you factor in these fees, you can't beat it. The issue, for them, is exceeding this very high cost."

Evensky believes that it is very difficult to beat the system. Like Charlie Ellis, who wrote Evensky's favorite investment book, "How to Win the Losers Game," Evensky believes that you win a loser's game by not losing. It's been over 20 years since Ellis, a respected researcher and consultant who has the ear of Wall Street, wrote that investing, like amateur tennis, had become a loser's game: The winners win not by splendid volleys and terrific backhands, but simply by making fewer mistakes than their opponents. To win at money management, "be sure you are playing your own game," Ellis wrote. "Know your policies very well and play according to them all the time." Second, Ellis said: Keep it simple. Bring turnover down. Concentrate on what you should see rather than what you should buy. "Most of the problems you will have in the next year are already in your portfolio," Ellis wrote.

Ellis' argument argues for passive management. So does Evensky. Yet Evensky still uses active management. About two-thirds of his portfolios are actively managed. Naturally, he tries to find managers who can best the indexes. But there are other, psychological reasons to use them, too, even if you don't think they can beat the system. "With active management, your client's a player," Evensky says. "Your clients can have a manager they can talk about. It's exciting. That's a legitimate reason to include active managers. The investor is likely to feel brilliant but never abused. If they lose in passive management, they are likely to feel dumb. If they lose with an active manager, the manager is dumb."

Still, it's hard to make an argument for an entirely actively managed portfolio, Evensky says. "How many Buffetts and Lynchs are there in the world?" he asks. "Can you find one in every asset class and style?" And simply choosing passive management does not mean your job is over, he warns. You must choose which index to use. You must decide whether the fund is doing a good job of following that index. "Passive funds are managed by real people who are making active philosophical decisions," he says. "There is room for both in your portfolio. Deciding how to use them is a process you must go through."

> *"We get concerned when a manager does great when their benchmark loses money. It says they're doing something they shouldn't be doing."*
>
> — HAROLD EVENSKY

As for him, Evensky uses four basic screens to pick managers.

◆ **Screen 1** eliminates what Evensky calls "inappropriate managers." "There are a lot of things we don't like," he says. "If we don't like them, we don't go any further." Out goes the manager. That includes managers who buy asset classes that Evensky doesn't want to use, those who use hedging techniques he doesn't like, or anything else that doesn't suit him. He has a list of asset classes and sub-asset classes, and he is looking for pure plays on these classes. For example, he doesn't buy global funds, because he wants to make the foreign/domestic allocation himself. He doesn't buy sector funds or junk bond funds or long-term bond funds. "We try to break our managers into philosophical pieces," he says. He wants managers who represent pure asset classes. In fixed income, he uses four different maturities and looks for managers to represent each one. For international bond funds, he wants one hedged fund and one unhedged fund.

Here, Evensky also looks at concentration. Any fund with sector weightings of more than three times those in the S&P 500 gets tossed. So does an international fund that has more than 135 percent of the EAFE index weighting in any one country or more than 150 percent of the Japanese weighting in Japan. "That still gives our managers plenty of leeway," Evensky says. "We don't want specialty funds or closet sector funds."

He looks, too, at the Morningstar style boxes to make certain that a manager is consistent in his style. But he ignores the star rating system. "They do an inappropriate job because they're too generalized," he says of the star ratings. "They're about as useful as the covers of *Money* magazine." And he makes his own decisions on what are large-cap, median-cap, and small-cap funds. "Using these screens narrows down my universe," Evensky says. "I eliminate a lot of very fine managers. But I only have one lifetime, and I can't examine every single mutual fund."

◆ **Screen 2** eliminates "fatal flaws." These include funds with expenses that are too high. Evensky screens out all domestic funds with expense ratios higher than 1.2 percent, international funds higher than 1.5 percent, and emerging-markets funds that are higher than 2 percent. He also looks at performance for the first time here. "We've all heard that past performance is no predictor of future performance," he says. "But past lousy performance probably is a good predictor of future performance." In fact, there is some good research that indicates that bad performance is almost always tied to high expenses. So a fund that's been in the bottom half for five years or the bottom third for three years gets tossed.

Fund capitalization comes up on this screen, too. "How much money the fund has is not really the issue," Evensky says. "Our concern is the growth of the fund assets." For example, Fidelity Magellan was achieving double-digit returns until it hit $2 billion in assets in 1985. "Then it was a totally different fund," Evensky says. "When we see that kind of asset growth, it makes us nervous." He eliminates funds that have grown 600 percent or more in the last year. Nor does he like hot funds with hot money. Evensky points to one volatile fund that attracted and lost investor money each time it went up and down. "Every time the fund did great, the money went into it," he says. "It did horrible, the money went out. It's a classic pattern, and we're particularly afraid of this kind of fund—not of the manager. I could live with that kind of volatility. But I'm petrified that my manager will be forced to sell in an illiquid market at the wrong time." Those funds are screened out.

He doesn't buy funds with brand-new managers, either. He looks for a manager with a minimum of three years in the job, but prefers five. "If we can track him somewhere else, that's OK," he says. And he doesn't like high turnover. "We're not concerned about taxes," he says. "But we're concerned with trading costs and spread. We think the manager won't be able to overcome the trading costs."

◆ **Screen 3** looks at the three Ps: philosophy, process, and people. By this time Evensky has narrowed down the thousands of available funds to a dozen or so in each of his asset classes. Now he is ready to dig in and look at each fund. "Now I've got a dozen small-cap growth managers to look at, and I can afford to devote some pretty good time and energy to looking at them." What he wants is a manager who is going to tell him in very specific terms why he should hand over some of his clients' money. "We want a credible story," Evensky says, "not 'I buy low and sell high.'"

What he wants is a manager with passion: someone with a unique and consistent style who will stick to his guns through thick and thin. One example he offers here is Don Yachtman. Evensky says he was impressed with Yachtman and was about to buy Selected American Shares some years ago when Yachtman was managing it. Yachtman had been on all the magazine covers as manager of the year. But that was not what impressed Evensky. What he liked was Yachtman's consistent style. Just as he was about to put his money in, Yachtman left to start his own fund, the Yachtman Fund, in 1992. "We didn't put money in the first year, because a new fund has a small asset base and high expenses," Evensky says. That turned out to be good luck on Evensky's part. "He had a disastrous first year," Evensky says. Now the magazines that had anointed him as manager of the year wanted to know what happened. And Yachtman was featured again. Evensky read the interviews. Yachtman told the press that he didn't know what happened. But he certainly had no intention of changing his style. "I'm doing what I did and that's what I'm going to keep doing," Yachtman said. "I don't know what happened, but I'm not going to change anything." That's just what Evensky wanted to hear. "That's my kind of manager," he said, and invested his clients' money. Yachtman has proved him right.

Once he knows that the manager has a consistent philosophy—a passion—Evensky wants to know what process he will use to carry it out. "How are you going to do this?" he wants to know. "Where do you get your research? How are you going to compensate your people? What's your bogey? How do you develop new ideas?" He doesn't care how much money the management team earns. But he wants to know what drives them. How long have they been there? Are they encouraged to share with each other? How do they determine buys and sells? How do they control trading costs?

Finally, he wants to know what kind of people are in the organization. "I don't want to have the person with passion leave and have a bunch of green-eyeshade bookkeepers left," he says. One way he learns about the people is to read the firm's marketing materials to see how they present themselves and what kind of image they want to project. "They spend a lot of money on this," Evensky says. "You can learn something here." He also saves all the old Value Line reports, and he refers to the Morningstar analysts' reports, which are collected in a library on Morningstar OnDisc. He networks with other planners, particularly those in the Alpha Group during their regular conference calls. He asks the managers he has selected to fill in a questionnaire, and, finally, he calls and talks with the manager. "We don't want someone who's selling us on a story," Evensky says. "We reject pomposity, simplicity, and marketing hype. We look for the nitty-gritty."

Part of the research comes from reading the prospectus. "It is your responsibility to read the prospectus completely," he says. Look carefully at the expense ratio. "There is frequently a footnote that says the managers are absorbing a portion of the expenses," he said. Watch out for this. "If one of your criteria is a maximum number for expenses, that might have fallen under your radar screen," he says. "Maybe you don't look at that footnote, and then six months later they drop this offer, and you are sitting with a fund that has much higher expenses than you ever anticipated."

Read the investment objectives, too, even though you can't expect to learn much here. "One of the problems with the prospectus now is that most fund companies are requesting permission to do anything," Evensky says. So you won't learn much about what they actually do—only what they are permitted to do. Do pay attention to the two kinds of investment policies, though: fundamental policies and general policies. This is legal terminology. Fundamental policies cannot be changed without going back to the shareholders and requesting a change. But nonfundamental policies can be changed by the board of directors. There is a trend for funds to sweep more changes into the nonfundamental category, where they can be easily made without going to shareholders. "It's important for you to know how much they can put into international, whether they can go on margin, and whether these things can be changed," Evensky says. "If these things can be changed without going back to a vote of the shareholders, you might not know until it's too late."

> *"Using these screens narrows down my universe. I eliminate a lot of very fine managers. But I only have one lifetime, and I can't examine every single mutual fund."*
>
> —HAROLD EVENSKY

Obtain and read the statement of additional information, too. This is a supplemental piece of information available by request from the fund company. It offers more detailed information on the trustee board members and 5 percent shareholders. "If you have an investment in REITs (real estate investment trusts), you might want to know who the big shareholders are, and if they might sell out for reasons of their own," Evensky says.

Look at the annual and quarterly reports. "It goes without saying that you should be reviewing those," Evensky says. He looks carefully at the manager's letter. "It's not that they're going to disclose something unique here," he says. "But it might just be namby-pamby and not say much of anything, like, 'We'd love to have your money, and we're going to do wonderful things for you.'" That is significant warning that this is not the kind of manager Evensky is looking for. "Managers with passion don't write namby-pamby letters," he says. "They tell you what they're doing. They tell you they really blew it that year and why they think they did and what they're going to do next year."

◆ **Screen 4** looks at performance. It's important here to select your performance benchmark carefully. You shouldn't care about how a fund performed relative to the S&P 500 unless it's a large-cap fund. "If it has nothing to do with the S&P in terms of philosophy and process, why would I care how it compares in performance?" It's important to explain to clients why the

Limited Opportunities

MOST FINANCIAL ADVISORS SAY they will not consider limited partnerships as investments for their clients. That's largely because of all the blowups in this area in the 1980s, but also because the partnerships are illiquid and difficult to analyze.

Bob Willard sees that as an opportunity. Willard does not use mutual funds. But he is eager to use both limited partnerships and direct real-estate investments. "My due diligence is more on direct lending and direct investing in real estate, oil, and gas," Willard says. "I paid a very painful tuition in the '80s, and now I want to cash in on it. This market is wide-open right now. There are some phenomenal deals. I've gotten very good at it."

Willard believes the real value of a planner is the ability to go beyond mutual funds. "As financial planners, we are often called upon to make recommen-

fund's relative performance is unimportant, too. "Tell clients you're not looking at that, and they should not, either," he says. Instead, he wants to know how the manager did compared to a benchmark that reflects that fund's objective. Of course, he'd like to see over-performance of that benchmark. But he also wants to know that the manager is following his mandate. That means he loses money when the benchmark does. "We get concerned when a manager does great when their benchmark loses money," he says. "It says they're doing something they shouldn't be doing."

What Evensky ends up with after he completes his due diligence is a list of approved managers—he generally has about 30. A manager stays on this list as long as he or she is consistent. Evensky is very patient with underperformance. The manager is allowed to under-

dations about other investments that are not in the conventional financial assets realm, but that involve real-estate investments," he says, "or that involve venture capital investments, things that are housed today in limited partnerships."

Due diligence on direct investments can make a big difference in a client's pocketbook. "If they're going to buy their own office building or medical practice building or invest in a surgery center, they really need your advice," he says.

And Willard does it in depth. "We do credit checks, we do background checks, we hire private detectives, we find out where their residences are, make sure there've been no name changes," Willard says. "That's the individual side." On the macro side, he does research on the markets, the economy, and the specific market his client will invest in.

perform for three quarters with no repercussions. After four quarters of underperformance, the fund goes on the "under review" list. He still sticks with these funds. But he watches them carefully. And now he begins to call other planners and open discussions about the fund to see what the problem is. "He might just be in the wrong place at the wrong time," Evensky says. "The last thing we want to do is fire a really good manager."

Another year of underperformance moves the manager to the "watch list." Evensky doesn't sell the fund. But he doesn't add new money, either. "There are a lot of problems with changing funds," he says. "We don't like to change." A fund might stay on the watch list for another year. "So it's roughly one year on the review list and one year on the watch list," he says. Finally, he has a wait list. These are managers that he likes but won't add to the list until someone else leaves.

Not every planner will agree with Evensky's due diligence process. But every planner should develop a disciplined process of his own for deciding what investment classes to use and which mutual funds best represent those classes. All the research in the process should be documented. "The process will continue to evolve," says Tim Kochis, "and we are all part of the process by continuing to identify to our clients, and to ourselves and to our colleagues, different ways, better ways, of thinking about the client and how to optimize wealth."

CHAPTER

BRINGING IN
CLIENTS

8

BEST PRACTICE Define the type of client you want to work with. Build a professional referral network to attract them. Work with the press or hold issue-oriented seminars to raise your visibility.

When Kyra Hollowell Morris was approaching the ten-year mark in her financial planning practice at the end of 1995, she realized it was adrift. Like most planners, she had spent the early years working hard to bring clients on board. Now she had plenty of them. But her fees were too low, and she wasn't making enough money. "I was frantically busy," Morris says. "I didn't have to look for clients. But it just didn't seem like I was profitable." Morris decided that she needed to restructure her business. So she started with a business plan that would lead her to the clients she wanted. "I realized that I was unfocused," Morris says now. "I was attempting to work for anybody who walked in the door." Out of her business plan came a marketing plan to target those clients she wanted. That included building a referral network, offering client seminars, and working with the press.

> *"Eighty percent of our*
> *marketing time is spent with*
> *existing clients because we all*
> *work so hard to get a client, and*
> *you don't want to lose one."*
>
> — D A V I D   B U G E N

Every successful planner has arrived at this crossroads. They've worked as hard as they could to establish their competence, their reputation, and a client list. Suddenly they realize they have all three. But they don't necessarily have the *type* of client they want to work with. When a planning practice is busy and growing, it can be difficult to tell whether it is successful. But most planners, like Morris, have realized that marketing is not just about attracting clients. It is about attracting the clients that are right for your business. "When you're starting out, you take any warm body that comes in the door," says Mary Malgoire. "But as you grow, you see that there is a kind of person you want to work with that matches the services you want to deliver."

Good marketing means creating a top-drawer image with potential clients, with other professionals like lawyers, accountants, and insurance agents. And with business reporters. That can take years. It requires lots of patience and a strategy.

The first step is to define who you are and what service you will provide. Many planners do that by specializing. Others decide that what they enjoy most is comprehensive financial planning. Either way, they target the type of client that they want to work with. Cynthia Meyers writes a business plan that is really an autobiography of sorts, incorporating the story of her life and the story of her business. That helps her focus on who she is and what type of client she will work well with. Then she adds her own action plan that will help her develop the business.

Here are some tips on developing a marketing strategy:

◆ **Don't open the door every time someone knocks.** This may sound elitist. But it's part of every good business practice. "You can't spend two hours with every potential client, or you won't get any work done," says Ron Rogé. "So as your clientele develops, you develop a niche market that you'd like to serve. You build your business plan around that, and you set your fees around that market." Other planners agree. "We have read so much about the 80/20 principle," says Jim Budros, "with 20 percent of our clients giving us 80 percent of our business and fees and referrals." Budros' firm is trying to do something about that. When the firm takes on a new client, "we try to figure out a way to get rid of a client from the lower 20 percent within the next six months," he says.

Similarly, Marilyn Capelli chats with a prospective client on the phone before inviting him or her into the office. "I tell them that I'm very selective about who we take on as clients," she says. "And then they tell me what a good prospect they are and ask if I would consider taking them on." This is sort of the Huck Finn approach. But it serves to screen out some of the clients that Capelli doesn't want.

◆ **Focus on existing clients.** It might seem pretty obvious, but good clients bring more good clients. "Eighty percent of our marketing time is spent with existing clients because we all work so hard to get a client, and you don't want to lose one," says David Bugen. Think about the impression your business makes on clients from the time they walk in the door or call you on the phone. "You market at every stage of the game," says Mary Malgoire. "Whatever they see while they're waiting for you to walk into the conference room is marketing. And everything you do with that client is marketing. So marketing is actually the entire business service you are providing." As Stuart Kessler says, "Most of our good clients come from our good clients. You do a good job for a client, and they're the best billboard there is."

◆ **Don't advertise.** Most financial advisors come to planning from a sales job. One of the first things the good ones learn is to leave their sales hat at the door. "The salesy stuff never works in financial planning," says Roy Diliberto, who came from an insurance background. "I don't think advertising ever works," adds Sharon Rich. "I have one ad that I've kept in a paper for 12 or 13 years, and I realized when I was renewing it recently that I do it simply because I like to support that paper. But as a marketing tool, I doubt that the ad has even paid for itself."

◆ **Follow your passion.** One of the best ways to target your audience is to hew to your interests and strengths. For Tim Kochis, a lawyer who had worked as a financial planning specialist in the corporate world, that led to working with corporate executives. Cicily Carson Maton, a Chicago-area planner, gravitated toward working with divorcing couples largely because she wanted to help others avoid some of the mistakes she felt she'd made in her own divorce.

Cynthia Meyers and George Kinder get involved in all aspects of a client's life—marriage, kids, career— in what they call lifestyle or life-cycle planning. Making certain the client has enough money to eke out an existence—or even live comfortably—in retirement is not enough for them. These two planners want to know what the client dreams about and what his regrets are. "If you died tomorrow, what would you most regret not having done?" Kinder asks a new client. And then they set to work on how to avoid that regret.

Myra Salzer works with inheritors—people who have inherited enough money that they never need to work again. Salzer sees herself as an advocate for this group, whom she realizes generally don't get much sympathy. Sharon Rich has a passionate interest in the obstacles women face when they try to deal with money. She specializes in working with women and money.

Bill Howard's interest in doctors led him to work with them almost exclusively. "I know a lot of planners don't like working with physicians," Howard says. "But I really enjoy it, especially those who are 65 and over." Once Howard identified doctors as his target market group, he approached the local medical society about writing a financial column for the newsletter. The editor agreed. That opened an opportunity to conduct financial planning seminars for members. "They do the mailings, and we coordinate the seminars with their attorney and CPA," Howard says.

The seminars have led to other speaking opportunities with physicians' groups. Howard has also made an effort to work with trade publications like *Medical Economics* and *Medical News*. As a result, his practice is booming. "Physicians have a lot of similar needs, and it's more effective for me to be able to deal with clients who have the same symptoms and to kind of leverage my time," Howard says. Specializing builds a solid referral network, too. "When you start working with

BEST PRACTICES FOR FINANCIAL ADVISORS

physicians, they tend to follow each other, so you get referrals from others," Howard says.

Pursuing your passion doesn't mean you must specialize. Many of these planners do comprehensive financial planning. But they have followed their interests and their instincts to give their practice a special twist, a unique niche. Then it is much easier to define your ideal client and to get attention.

◆ **Don't bother with a newsletter.** Sure, it's a broad generalization, and there are some outstanding exceptions. But newsletters require a lot of work. A bad one can do as much harm as good. A newsletter is worth the effort only if you intend to invest the time to do a really top-notch job and to offer clients information they cannot get elsewhere. One issue of Cynthia Meyers' monthly newsletter comes to mind here. Meyers, who was an editor of children's books in an earlier career, writes well. And she used this newsletter to discuss the importance of using an advisor to help your kids find the right college and to get accepted there—a real hot button with parents. Unless you're willing to do the research to provide something novel like that, your time can be better spent elsewhere.

Many planners say they have tried—and abandoned—newsletters. Those who find them worthwhile typically use them to educate clients. For example, Mary Malgoire, who published a newsletter but abandoned it years ago, revisited the issue in 1996 and decided to put together an educational bulletin reiterating the importance of diversification and asset allocation. "We want to make sure they stay with us through the next crash," she says. Simply reporting on the various industry conferences you attended is not worthwhile.

Instead of a newsletter, Kyra Morris sends personal notes to keep the lines of communication open with clients. Morris got the idea from her mentor, a gentleman in his eighties, who calls it a "nurturing plan." She buys high-quality, tasteful cards. "My mentor told me you really have to pick out a card that has some class," she says. "He sent me some examples, such as those from the Metropolitan Museum of Art or historical etchings of Charleston."

> *When the firm takes on*
> *a new client, "we try to figure*
> *out a way to get rid of a client*
> *from the lower 20 percent*
> *within the next six months."*
>
> —JIM BUDROS

He also helped her with the greetings. "He told me not to say something like 'so-and-so on the staff is pregnant,'" Morris says, but to give a personalized report of what is going on in the economy or the stock market or what the client's portfolio is doing, as well as a personal thought. The message is just a couple of lines long, with a signature. Results have been dramatic. One of her clients, who had a particularly gruff exterior, has totally changed in his attitude toward her. "Now I'm his long-lost daughter," Morris says.

Several planners also reported success with a Thanksgiving letter. "We send out a letter thanking our clients for their business, and we used to ask for referrals as they're meeting with family and friends around the holidays," Ron Rogé says. "Handwritten lists would come in with names of family and friends." Rogé doesn't ask for referrals anymore because he's too busy. But he still sends the letter. Marilyn Capelli sent Thanksgiving letters for the first time in 1995. "It was nothing more than a letter on pretty paper," she says, "but we had a great response."

◆ **Build a referral network.** Many planners say professional referrals are their best source of new clients. "We track where all of our referrals come from, and about 50 percent come from CPAs," says David Homrich. "I trained as a CPA, and so we play to our strength, and we've made a point to be very active in the personal financial-planning committee in the Georgia Society of CPAs." When Kyra Morris developed her new marketing plan, she knew that working with other professionals was key. Her goal was to meet two new people each week. "It might be a tax attorney or, because we're a resort community, it might be a real-estate developer," Morris said. Sharon Rich, a fee-only planner who does not manage money, schedules regular lunches with stockbrokers, insurance agents, and others whom she will exchange referrals with.

Making contacts is only the first step. Building a network is a critical second step. For example, David Bugen concentrates on a small group of professionals. "If you try to work with 30 people, it's not going to work out," Bugen says. "If you work with two or three attorneys, two or three accountants, and two or three insurance agents, then you can develop a better rapport with them, and you can give them referrals. Of course, there's no quid pro quo, but the fact of the matter is, if you do something for someone else, they're going to recognize that and be more responsive to you." Working with a small group helps everyone get comfortable with the competence of the others. "When they refer you to someone, their reputation is at stake, and they want to get to know you and make sure that you do a quality job," Bugen says. Sending thank-you cards is helpful, too. Cynthia Meyers sends a personal handwritten note to anyone who refers a client to her. Many professionals keep track of where their business comes from. "I work with one accounting firm that sends me a letter every six months," Bugen says. "They say: 'In the last six months, you sent us X number of referrals. Thank you very much.'"

◆ **Don't ignore professional groups.** When Diahann Lassus started out as a planner a decade ago, she and her partner made the decision to create name recognition for their firm as a fee-only financial planning firm. She joined NAPFA as well as the ICFP and the National Organization of Women Business Owners. She sits on a number of boards. "The drive was to get our name out there," she says, "and we've continued to do that." The strategy has been extremely effective, Lassus says. Activity in professional groups and the name recognition that it's brought have resulted in frequent requests to appear on radio and television programs.

Members of NAPFA swear by the referrals that 500-member group provides. When consumers contact NAPFA for the names of local planners, they are sent several names, as well as a brochure on how to interview a planner. At the same time, NAPFA sends the planners the names of these prospective clients. Most NAPFA members respond to those consumers. Lassus sends "a pretty elaborate package," including reprints of articles about the firm, résumés of the principals, and the company brochure.

Because he gets nearly 100 names a month, Rogé sends only a letter with a postcard that the prospective client can return to get the full packet. "We only do that to save money, because it is a $3 mailing," he says.

◆ **Consider seminars.** Planners report good success with educational seminars for clients or other professionals. "The only marketing we've done for the general public that has worked for us is seminars," says Roy Diliberto. Diliberto says he tried a number of methods of publicizing the seminars. What worked best was inserts in *The Philadelphia Inquirer,* his local newspaper, that targeted specific areas of the metropolitan region.

He buys specific zones on a Thursday and inserts an 8½" x 11" sheet advertising a seminar on retirement or building a winning portfolio of no-load mutual funds.

> *"Physicians have a lot of similar needs, and it's more effective for me to be able to deal with clients who have the same symptoms and to kind of leverage my time."*
>
> — BILL HOWARD

Initially, he offered a free hour of consultation to anyone who attended the seminar. But he ended up with a lot of takers who were not good candidates as clients. "Now we tell them our minimums at the seminar, so that serves to weed them out," he says. Of course, he will still give a free consultation to anyone who signs up for one. But prospective clients know whether they are candidates for the firm or not. Current clients send friends to the seminars, too. "It is a very, very nonthreatening way of referring people, because they can say: 'Go to a seminar. If you like what you hear, go see him. If not, you haven't lost anything.'" Between 30 and 50 people attend a seminar, and Diliberto typically picks up two clients.

Bob Winfield uses seminars to demonstrate his competence to other professionals. The seminars, which might deal with the Uniform Prudent Investor Act or ERISA law, provide continuing-education credits for attorneys and certified public accountants. He charges "just enough to cover the cost, so it's a very cheap credit." For the professionals who come, "it tends to solidify those relationships, because when you stand there answering questions from the floor on different matters, it becomes apparent if you know what you're talking about," Winfield says.

Myra Salzer sponsors workshops for inheritors to talk about issues surrounding money and relationships. Although the seminars are a great deal of work, they have helped to plug her into the network. She also speaks to groups of therapists, for example, on the issues and problems facing people with inherited wealth and works to sensitize others to the special problems faced by people who don't really need to work for a living. "This has certainly helped me to define the niche," she says.

Finally, David Bugen offers a series of luncheons for existing clients. "We'll have it in a room at a club that will hold 25 people, and we'll eat lunch for an hour and then have a speaker who is a portfolio manager or an expert on the tax law," Bugen says. Bugen does the luncheons five times a year. He polls clients to see what they want to hear about. For example, he planned one seminar for people with most of their assets in their qualified plans that tried to answer this question: How do you combine estate planning and income-tax planning when you have little in the way of personal resources outside a retirement plan? Luncheons are first-come, first-served. "They can bring a friend if they wish," Bugen says. In addition to providing a benefit to existing clients—and occasionally getting new clients—Bugen uses the seminars to cement referral relationships with the experts he invites to speak. "We're a small firm here in New Jersey, and there are probably 15 brokerage houses within a mile of our office," he says. "We want to do something special to be responsive to the needs of our clients."

◆ **Don't ignore the press.** The press has power. Consider what the business press has done for NAPFA and for fee-only planners in general. By telling consumers that fee-only planners are better for them, the business press has virtually ensured that fee-only planners represent the future. NAPFA members happily rode that wave.

And NAPFA has done other things to keep reporters happy, too. For example, NAPFA set up a centralized clearinghouse to help reporters find consumers they need for a particular story. To hook into the network, a reporter faxes a description of what he's looking for, and the chair of the public relations committee faxes that on to the committee's seven members. Each of them passes the description on to six or seven planners in their area. "We can see by articles in places like *Money* magazine that this is working," Rogé says. As a reporter who often needs names of investors to interview, I can assure you that this is a successful strategy.

Some planners might decide not to work with the press. But the press can't be ignored. In October 1994, *Worth* magazine named 60 top advisors in an article called "A Skeptical Guide to Financial Advisors." The planners on that list said that cooperating with *Worth* was the best piece of marketing work they had ever done. "The best exposure I've gotten was the *Worth* magazine listing," says Stuart Kessler, who is a partner at a CPA firm in New York. "That resulted in a number of good clients. But more than that, I was able to convince my partners that we needed to build up our financial planning department, because it's important."

Remember that a list like *Worth*'s has ripple effects that go on for years. Reporters clip it and use it when they need to contact a financial planner. For example, Sharon Rich participates in a money-makeover series for *The Boston Globe* that she says came to her because she was on the *Worth* list. *Worth* did a second article—"The Best Financial Advisers"—in October 1996. Cynthia Meyers reported the same level of inquiries from this expanded list of 200. Not only did she get a number of calls from potential clients, but other reporters—including one at her local newspaper—followed up with their own stories.

Everybody in business wants to appear on a list like the one published by *Worth* or to be quoted favorably in *The New York Times* and *The Wall Street Journal.* But getting any kind of mention in these publications usually doesn't happen until you've invested years in building your reputation and cooperating with every reporter who calls you. Working with the press requires commitment. Reporters are demanding. Some are arrogant and rude. They are nearly always on deadline. They want an answer immediately when they call. If you are not available, they will move on to someone who is. You might decide that working with the press is too much trouble. But if you are truly committed to working with reporters, here is some advice on how to do it:

◆ **Give reporters a priority that is one notch above your best client.** Return phone calls immediately, even if you are on the road. "I give reporters my home number if they want to reach me on the weekend," Stu Kessler says. Inform your secretary to put reporters through when the call comes in. "I never turn down a call from *The Washington Post,*" says Mary Malgoire.

But don't underestimate the time it will take. You might spend several hours with a reporter. Then you're likely to get several call-backs to recheck facts. Finally, magazines use fact checkers. So when the story is done—and you've completely forgotten about it—a fact checker will call you to go over everything again. Once you've bought into the process, you have to hang in there. "I do get upset sometimes when I'm called back three or four times and then a fact checker calls me and goes over everything again," Kessler says. "But I try to take it all in good spirits. The minute you show irritation, that person is going to strike you from their list."

◆ **Say something quotable.** Take a stand. Reporters like sources who are willing to be controversial.

◆ **Remember that it's OK to ask to schedule an interview later.** For instance, if you feel you need to do research, or you simply don't have the time at the moment, ask if there's time to schedule a later interview. Take the interview seriously. Do your research. List the points you want to make. Be punctual. Always have a summation prepared. Make it punchy and quotable.

> *"We'll have [client luncheons]*
>
> *in a room at a club that*
>
> *will hold 25 people*
>
> *and have a speaker who*
>
> *is a portfolio manager or an*
>
> *expert on the tax law."*

— DAVID BUGEN

◆ **Never ask to see the story before it is published.** That is strictly bush. Reporters at top publications would never show their finished work to a source. By asking to see it, you show that you haven't had much experience working with reporters.

◆ **Work on building relationships with reporters.** Most reporters work hard to develop knowledgeable sources in the areas they cover. A reliable, available source is very valuable. They will keep coming back to you. If you are called about a subject that is outside your bailiwick, refer the reporter to someone who is strong in that area.

◆ **Troll for story ideas.** Be on the lookout for situations that could make a good 1,000-word story. That's about four typewritten pages, and it is the ideal length for personal finance columns. A personal finance column takes a strong point of view. It typically needs three points to bolster the conclusion.

The best ideas come from changes in tax laws or from obscure planning situations. Internal Revenue Service private letter rulings can make good stories. So can an everyday situation faced by a client. For example, suppose you see a client who wants to buy a second home. Think about the considerations that go into the decision-making process. List the pros and cons in a concise manner and send them to a reporter. It's best to do this with someone you have a relationship with—or that you've at least met. You need to establish your credibility before you begin suggesting stories.

◆ **Don't be afraid to pass on a story idea that you don't like.** It's usually fairly easy to divine the reporter's agenda. If you don't like it, don't participate. Or make it clear that you don't agree. Suppose you get a call from a reporter working on a story on Medicaid planning—or planning to protect assets for the family while one member goes on Medicaid. It's a legitimate planning strategy. But maybe you think it's morally wrong. Say so. And be quotable about it. Or maybe the story idea is timing the market, and you don't believe it can be done. Say so. And say why. "Someone called me at the end of the year and wanted a quote about what was going to happen to the market in the new year," says Sharon Rich. "I passed on that one real quick."

◆ **Don't try to control the reporter.** It's OK to make your point forcefully. But don't expect to talk the reporter into it. It's also OK to check out the reporter—or the agenda—before you talk. For example, Myra Salzer won't talk to reporters about her clients—who are inheritors—until she gets a sense of what approach the reporter plans to take. "I have been careful in working with a reporter in terms of how they will frame the inheritance challenges," she says. "If they're going to be flip or take the 'poor little rich person' approach, I won't work with them."

◆ **Remember that reporters love to talk to real people.** Think about how you will handle that. If you have a client with an interesting situation who is willing to talk to a reporter, that can be a gold mine. But tread carefully when you get a call asking for a client.

"I'm asked that question all the time," says David Homrich. "There was only one situation where I felt I had a proper fit. It was for *The Wall Street Journal,* and I told the client: 'Let me tell you the reasons why you should do it and the reasons why you shouldn't do it.'" Homrich pointed out that it would help the article get published, "which is in my best interest, but not necessarily yours." The client ultimately decided not to do it.

David Bugen had a client who wanted to talk to a magazine that was working on a story about 403(b) plans. She had invested her 403(b) money in an insurance company that ran into trouble. "She was an elderly lady who worked at a hospital, and she was asked to send in a picture," Bugen recalls. "The magazine told her that she was not photogenic enough, and she was very upset." Tim Kochis has decided that he will never offer clients' names. "It comes up over and over," Kochis says. "There are just too many negatives."

◆ **Don't waste your time—and damage your credibility—suggesting sweeping story ideas.** Reporters know about the obvious stuff, such as "Most people simply do not save enough money for retirement," or "Many Americans pay too much in taxes." Don't send a letter pointing out that you are an expert in a particular area, either. That is a real turn-off. You'll have to prove that yourself.

◆ **Work with trade publications.** Many professionals

mistakenly believe that because consumers do not read trade publications, it is a waste of time to work with them. The truth is that reporters from the top consumer publications like *The New York Times, The Los Angeles Times,* and *The Wall Street Journal* read trade publications. They are always looking for new sources and new story ideas. If a planner—or any type of professional—is featured prominently in such a publication, reporters will take note of it. It is one of the best ways to get instant visibility and credibility.

◆ **Introduce yourself to local reporters.** When Malgoire started working as a financial planner in the Washington, D.C., area, she called Al Crenshaw at *The Washington Post* and invited him to lunch. "He wouldn't let me pay for his lunch," said Malgoire, "which I thought was honorable. But we chitchatted and had a nice time." A profile in a local newspaper can be very valuable. "One of my biggest sources of clients was a profile the local newspaper did of me," says Cynthia Meyers. The profile included a photo of Meyers with a client. Meyers got 16 calls as a result. Every one of the callers became a client.

◆ **Treat every publication with respect.** You never know when a reporter will move from a publication you find insignificant to *The Wall Street Journal.* Don't brush anyone off. Remember, too, that press coverage has a ripple effect. The more you're quoted, the more you'll *be* quoted. "Most reporters call me because they've seen me quoted somewhere before," Kessler says. "It's like if you get a lot of calls, that means you'll get a lot more calls."

◆ **Expect *something* in exchange for your time.** Don't badger the reporter with repeated calls asking when the article will run, how many times you'll be quoted, etc. If you want to be quoted, you should give freely of your time and then leave it at that. However, you should expect something to be attributed to you in an article. Perhaps you won't get as much as you expect. But it seems reasonable that busy people will not donate their time if they never get anything in exchange.

Here is the way I see it, as a reporter. There are not many people who really know their stuff and know how to explain it so that I can grasp it. If I interview someone who does not seem competent or is not quotable, I don't use the information, and I don't call them again. When I devour a great deal of someone's time and expertise, and that person is truly helpful in providing information I need, I make a real effort to get that person into the story. Even if the story is cut to fit, I will fight to include a source who has made a substantial contribution to the story. That only seems fair. If all reference to that person is cut from the final version of the story, I bend over backwards to use that source again.

A Grocery-Cart Campaign

WHEN KYRA MORRIS DEVELOPED a marketing plan to help target the clients she wanted to attract, she did all the right things. And then she did something unusual: She agreed to an ad campaign that would plaster her face and phone number on grocery shopping carts throughout her community near Charleston, South Carolina.

"That was a weak moment," Morris admits now. "This adorable guy came in. I'm sorry, but he really was adorable. I had just closed the retainer on one of my largest clients, and I was feeling so good."

The grocery-cart campaign was inexpensive—just $700. "It didn't dawn on me until later where it would appear," Morris says. When the salesman left, "I had this gut-wrenching feeling of, 'What have I done?'" Morris says. But she took it in stride. "I still don't totally regret it," she says. "I just made it into kind of a joke."

◆ **Collect all the press clippings that mention you and your practice.** If you want reprints, call the publication and ask about the reprint policy. Even if you plan to make them yourself, you need permission from the publication. Planners report good success with sending out reprints in their marketing package. "We found out that it gives you more credibility with a prospective client than your CFP or CPA designation or any other type of training," says Ron Rogé. "If we're quoted in *Money* magazine, we probably will not receive any calls. But when we send out the reprint to prospective clients, they will actually read the article and bring it up. Often, they think you wrote it yourself."

Many planners use press reprints in their reception room. Use good sense here, though. Think about whether the story really reflects well on you. I once

It may have loosened up her image a bit, too. Financial planners are seen as strait laced and conservative—people who get you to eat your prunes and save your quarters. Morris, who takes karate lessons three times a week and fills in as social director at industry functions like the ICFP Retreat, is anything but.

It clearly doesn't hurt for prospective clients to see her as human. It raised her visibility, too. A lot of people commented that they had seen her in the grocery store. "They said things like: 'I couldn't get away from you in the supermarket,'" Morris says.

So the grocery-cart campaign brought her a lot of attention and some laughs. But it probably didn't bring her the clients she wanted to target. "It made more of a splash than I ever thought," Morris says. "But it is definitely not target marketing. It is big-splash marketing."

wrote a column for *The New York Times* that mentioned a business problem faced by my dentist. The next time I went to his office, he had the column prominently displayed. It *did* show that he had been mentioned in *The New York Times*, but only because he was having a problem with his dental practice. That probably wasn't such a good marketing strategy. It was gone on my next visit.

> *"So as your clientele develops,*
>
> *you develop a niche*
>
> *market that you'd like to*
>
> *serve. You build your*
>
> *business plan around that."*
>
> — RON ROGÉ

WORKING
WITH CLIENTS

BEST PRACTICE Look for signs of distress when a new client approaches you. Try to determine why they need you now. Go beyond financial needs to get a sense of the whole person and what he or she hopes for and dreams of accomplishing. Then build a solid relationship with each client based on mutual trust and respect.

The relationship between a person and his money is complex, mysterious—and often secret. Psychologists call money the last frontier in therapy. "Sex was the most important area of conflict in Victorian times," says Boston psychiatrist John W. Schott. "Now, it's money."

Our society has institutionalized neurotic attitudes about money, says Schott, who, as chairman of the Department of Psychiatry at Metro West Medical Center in Boston, specializes in treating money-related disorders. "Every individual has a set of conflicts," he says. Think of money attitudes as stretching along a bell curve. Those who are in the middle have what Washington, D.C., psychotherapist Olivia Mellan calls "money harmony" in her book by that name. People with money harmony save, invest wisely, pay their bills on time, spend something on pleasure, give to charity, and rarely focus on what they don't have. On both ends of the curve are people who are seriously at odds with their money. And in between are the slightly dysfunctional.

Many of them erect intricate barriers around money issues. It is the job of a financial advisor to delicately dismantle these barriers and persuade a client to outline his dreams and his fears and the role that money plays in them. No matter how the planner does it, though, the process can be very threatening to many people. Money can represent power, love, sex, hope— all of the most powerful feelings a person confronts. When a professional delves into them, the result may be an explosion. "Working with a financial planner means delving into the most volatile of human conflicts," says Dr. William R. Nixon Jr., a psychoanalyst in Birmingham, Michigan.

How a planner handles this challenge has more to do with his ultimate success or failure than any other aspect of the planning process. Of all the topics covered in the roundtable discussions for this book, it was "working with clients" that generated the most interest. "This is what makes all the rest of what we do effective," says Diahann Lassus. "How good you are at dealing with your clients' expectations and helping them achieve their goals determines whether you will ultimately succeed."

That makes working with clients the toughest part of planning. Someone who is good with numbers can master the nuts and bolts of planning. But not every mathematician is a psychologist—and that's what a good planner is, at least in part. Yet working with clients is also the gratifying part of planning. It is one of the things that sets planning apart from sales. Sales is about selling something to fill a need—like a dishwasher or a mutual fund. Planning is about figuring out a way to fulfill dreams.

> *"How good you are at dealing with your clients' expectations and helping them achieve their goals determines whether you will ultimately succeed."*
>
> —DIAHANN LASSUS

"This is the area I enjoy the most and get the most satisfaction from," says Bill Howard. "It means watching people make progress toward their dreams." The progress may be mundane in its parts—paying off debt, tracking net worth, setting aside savings—but accomplishing it is something most clients simply could not do on their own, without a coach.

Once a relationship with a client is established, it can be pure magic. "People hire us for all sorts of reasons," says Roy Diliberto. "But people keep us because of the relationship." Most clients are so loyal they would never think of leaving a planner with whom they have built a good relationship. For example, Diahann Lassus was working with a couple that went through a divorce in 1996. One of their biggest issues was which partner would get Lassus as a planner. They worked it out so that she would continue to represent both.

Sometimes even the most difficult clients genuinely treasure the relationship. Consider a woman who had been a client of Judy Shine for ten years when the two had a falling out. Shine suggested that they part ways. But the client rebelled. "It is extremely difficult for me to open up about these very personal issues," the woman told her. "I have built a history with you. Even though I don't always agree with you, I feel comfortable with you. When you tell me that I'm out of here if I don't agree with you, I feel very, very badly." Shine backed off and continued to work with this woman.

Getting to the good part means negotiating some rocky shoals, though. Most clients come to a planner with plenty of baggage. If they could handle their own financial affairs, if they had no hangups around money, they wouldn't need you. A savvy planner has to be able to recognize danger signs—suspiciousness, distrust, paranoia—and separate them from what is often a natural and normal anxiety about money.

A client comes to a planner with a past. "You are not interacting with a clean slate," Nixon says. "The way a client deals with you is only partly to do with you and lots to do with what preceded you in their life." Talking about money can lay bare all the skeletons in the closet. It reminds the client about what money means to him and, perhaps, of all of the choices he has made around it. It might even resurrect dormant issues from childhood, Nixon says: Was mom at home? Was there enough money? What did dad do? Was money a source of tension and conflict? Money has a lot to do with why a client married the wife or husband they did, the success of their marriage, and how they are raising their children. That gives the planner a tough job. "If you have an intuitive sense about the human condition, you can be prepared for this," Nixon says.

For many people, dealing with money evokes conflicts surrounding dependency. "During the long period of time when we couldn't care for ourselves and
had to depend on our parents, we developed conflicts
about dependent needs," Nixon says. Most adults have
become independent. But many still have conflicts
about money that makes them feel dependent. When
a client comes to a planner for help with money, the
client typically transfers his feelings about a parent
onto the planner. "A client may have certain expectations of you that are impossible to meet," Nixon told a
group of planners at the ICFP Retreat in Traverse City,
Michigan, in July 1996. "When you interact with
clients, you are touching on a stage of adolescent
development." Like a teenager, the client may vacillate
between trying to help the planner and showing the
planner that he doesn't really need help. "If you keep
in mind that the experience is like working with a
teenager, if you are capable of withstanding it and
working through it, you will be able to get to the other
side," Nixon said, "which is the goal of parents who
have teenagers."

Many clients start out with unrealistic expectations
for the relationship, too. Some come to a financial
planner because they've heard about annual returns
of 20 or 30 percent, and they want to cash in on them.
It's your task to explain that financial planning means
much more than investing—and to explain what is
realistic in investment returns.

Some clients have even broader expectations. They
believe that the planner will right all the wrongs in
their lives. These clients resemble patients who go to
see a therapist. "Everyone who comes to see me
expects to visit two or three times and have their life
turned around," Nixon says. Similarly, when a client
comes in to see a planner, he may have had a marginal financial life. "Perhaps his wife thinks he's a loser,"
Nixon says. Maybe he can't hold a job. Bills are piling

up. "But after today," this client is likely to think, "things will be different. I'll have a Rolls-Royce, a place in Florida."

This is particularly true for planners with high visibility. "They expect you to change their lives," says Ginger Applegarth, a planner and author who appears frequently on the "Today" show and CNBC and is quoted widely in the media. "They give you this aura of complete infallibility."

> *"How do you tell somebody*
> *that it is a relationship they*
> *really want, when they think*
> *what they want is for you*
> *to beat the S&P 500?"*
>
> — ROY DILIBERTO

A new client might think a planner can help them mend their ways. For example, Applegarth sees one couple—both of whom have six-figure incomes—who told her, "Ginger, you've got to make us stop spending so much money." Others often expect the planner to mend family relationships, too. They might think a financial expert can turn a husband from spendthrift to saver. "People say, 'Talk to my husband and get him to do this or that,'" says Deena Katz. Or they're likely to think a planner can defuse emotional issues in the family. Sometimes they'll say, "Please talk to my children. I want them to understand why I want to cut them out of my will."

Planners need to listen carefully to clients when they talk about their needs. "As clients speak in this fashion, you should be beginning to put together a psychological profile of your clients," Nixon says. Make a list of the things you are looking for. For example, you want to know about a client's values, expectations, attitudes about money, concerns about family and the future, childhood experiences in working with money, failures, disappointments, the roads not taken, and the reason this person came in to see you now.

"Ask about parents, siblings, anything to get them to talk to you," Nixon suggests. "Everybody has a story; a past and a present. You can develop a psychological profile if you ask questions and listen." Listen carefully to everything the client says about the meaning of money in his life. And then be careful to respect his needs and his fears. "Until they trust you, you don't have a customer," Nixon says.

As you are working with a new client, remember that that person has probably tried many different things to solve his money problems before he decided to work with a planner. Of course you will want to know about some of those attempts—and why they failed. But you'll have to read between the lines. "There is no way anyone who comes to you is going to tell you the truth," Nixon says. "They'll tell you their best version of it."

Also look for signs of serious distress. The issues that people must confront with planners—mortality, lack of adequate resources, perhaps divorce—cause stress. "They may come to you to talk about planning a life with their spouse, when they feel ambivalent about that spouse," Nixon says. That can result in anger and hostility. "What you should know is that operating beneath the surface is anxiety," Nixon says.

Some clients may be operating beyond an acceptable level of stress, so planners should look for danger signs. They include hand tremors, shortness of breath, sweat across the forehead, avoidance of certain subjects. "You might be talking to them, and you can see that they refuse to land on a certain subject," Nixon says. Of course, you don't want to say: "My God, you're so anxious." Instead, Nixon suggests that a planner say: "You know, often when people speak to me they get anxious." Clients who are depressed show different signs: sleep problems, change in appetite, weight loss or gain, uncontrolled crying.

This is not to say that planners must be psychiatrists—although a basic understanding of psychology certainly helps. Nor does it mean that a planner must take on all clients who walk in the door. Most planners say that they initially did try to work with everyone. "Ten years ago, when I was starting my business, I was grateful for anyone I could get," says David Homrich. "There were times when I felt like I was taking on some clients where I just had to remind myself that I wasn't going to socialize with them, and I didn't have the respect for them I would have liked, but perhaps you have to compromise a little in the early going."

But that's not the case for Homrich—or the rest of these planners—anymore. Most of them say they know right off whether a client will be a good fit. "I have a gut feel for it right from the beginning," says Ginger Applegarth. "Every time I've gone against that feeling, I've paid—big time."

Planners at the top of their profession pick and choose. And that's as it should be. "I hope you don't take all the clients who come to you," Nixon says. "I would make a terrible mistake as a practitioner if I tried to work with everyone," he says. "So would you." For instance, Nixon says he does not take clients whose problems hold no interest for him. Or those that he feels unequipped to deal with. In the spring of 1996, when he and his wife were mourning the loss of one of their closest friends, a patient came for help in dealing with the death of a friend. "I couldn't help him," Nixon says. "It was not the time for me to deal with that patient."

Applegarth tells people on the phone, before they

come in, that she will schedule a meeting to discuss whether and how they might work together. If she doesn't click with the client, she tells them on the spot. She knows it will be a difficult conversation—but far easier than getting involved with someone whose demands she is not willing or able to meet. Mary Merrill fills out a 5" x 7" card while she talks with prospective clients on the phone, asking questions about their financial situation, exploring exactly what they are looking for, and detailing her fees. If she doesn't think the client is a good fit, she doesn't invite them in for a meeting.

Four Types

IN HIS 15 YEARS AS A FINANCIAL PLANNER, Ross Levin has identified four different kinds of clients. One type—the greedy client—is bad business. "All the pain I've had in this business has come from greedy clients," Levin says. "Typically, they have some unarticulated objectives that are almost always measured by short-term results. They are really hard to work with."

Greedy clients tend to be capricious, Levin says. "You don't know what they're after until it's too late. They come in for broad financial planning, but what they're really after is results." No matter what you do, a greedy client will never be happy, Levin says. "At first, I couldn't pick them out. But now, I can see them in the lobby." One tip-off is if they've moved around a lot in their professional relationships, he says.

Levin always asks clients: "If I were to do a good job, what would that look like to you?" The greedy client will always answer that a good job means "beating the market by 5 percent a year," Levin says. "The greedy client tends to believe that you can time the market." Levin says he won't take on greedy clients anymore. "The difference between me today and me ten years ago is that today I'll walk away from business."

The clients that make up the bulk of his business are relationship clients. These clients are "very trusting and defer to you on all decisions," Levin says. They want to feel comfortable, so they open up and share a lot of themselves. "If you spend an hour with them, 55 minutes will be spent talking about what's going on in their life and five minutes on business." The danger with relationship clients is that it is difficult to establish boundaries between business and personal life. "A lot of financial stuff will be driven by personal feelings," Levin says. The client might become so reliant on you that they don't monitor what you're doing. "If things go sour, they can't necessarily re-create what you're doing," Levin says. "It can create disharmony. With these clients, Levin says, he makes certain to summarize meetings on paper regularly, "so that they have something else but their memory to go on."

The third type are what Levin calls fear-based clients, which make up just a small part of his practice. These clients usually have had very little financial experience, or they've had bad financial experiences. Sometimes fear-based clients seem angry or withdrawn, "but underneath it is mostly worry," Levin says. He works with this type of client to educate him and help him get over his fear. The danger with this type of client is that you may not know what he's thinking or how anxious he is. Clients don't remain for long in this group. They either give up on investing or move to one of the other types. If he can educate them properly, Levin says, he can keep them as clients.

The fourth type is the curious client, who tends to be very knowledgeable about investing. "They come to the table with ideas and like to focus on items that validate their opinion," Levin says. "If they come up with the idea that Mexico is a great emerging market of the 21st century, they will bring all the articles that support their view. The negative ones get lost." Because they have such strong opinions, these clients tend to pull a portfolio in a particular direction. "They might think that this is the time to own only U.S. stocks," he says.

"The reason they're working with you is because of time constraints. It's not necessarily because they think you can do a better job." The danger with the curious client is that you will lose control of the investment process. "You must constantly readdress issues with them and make your point of view through articles that you find," he says. "They will be reading a ton of different things. You need to continually prove yourself."

"We don't really get to the investing for perhaps six months," Ruhlin says. It might take Bill Howard that long to get a plan in place, too. "We try to get people to see they need patience," he says.

— PEGGY RUHLIN,
BILL HOWARD

For most planners, the first meeting with a client is about getting to know each other. Many of them offer the initial consultation without charge. The planner is trying to learn who the client is and what he wants. Experts claim that most money problems involve distortions around four issues. The first is spending, with compulsive savers and compulsive spenders at the two extremes. The second is order, with the fretter who keeps a running tally of expenses on one hand and the procrastinator who doesn't pay bills on the other. Third comes risk, where we find avoiders and gamblers. And finally, morality: Misers worship money; puritans believe it taints them.

There are a number of ways to get at these issues in the first meeting. Judy Shine asks all prospective clients the same three questions: Why are you here? What is the greatest error you have ever made money-wise? What keeps you awake at night? She wants to know how the client feels about money as well as what he wants it to do for him. "We're trying to find a way to know our client well enough to do planning that fulfills what it is that they dream their life might be about," says George Kinder.

At the same time, the planner tries to reveal enough about himself to help the client feel comfortable and to know what to expect. "I tell them I am not a performance pig and that I believe in managing all aspects of net worth," Shine says. Client and planner talk. Client and planner listen. And they each decide whether this is a relationship that will work. "The initial interview is a minuet," says Ross Levin in his book, "Wealth Management Index." "The relationship develops almost rhythmically with two people carefully trying to gain confidence in each other."

Here are some of the other questions planners ask:

◆ **What brings you here?** "People don't pick up the phone and call a financial planner on a regular basis," Shine says. "So obviously, there is an impetus for you to be here. Tell me what it is."

◆ **Tell me about yourself.** Roy Diliberto asks all clients that same question. Then he lets them talk. "It's really interesting how people answer that question in so many different ways," he says. "Some people talk about their families; other people talk about their jobs." Ginger Applegarth carefully watches body language during this first meeting. "I look to see if there's some underlying tension around these issues," she says.

◆ **What do you think we can do for you?** "That's part of managing their expectations," says Deena Katz. "If we know up front exactly what they have in their minds, we can tell them: 'Yes, that's what we do' or 'No, we're not going to hire a maid for you.'"

◆ **What money messages did you get growing up?** "We are all creatures of our past, so this question allows people to discuss how their family background shaped their money profile," says Ross Levin.

◆ **If I were to do a good job for you, what would that be?** "We cannot minimize the original expectations," Levin says.

◆ **Where would you like to be in five years?**

◆ **How will you be involved in the process?** "This will help identify your client's profile and understand how they learn," Levin says.

◆ **What is important about money (or success) to you?** "Most clients have not really thought that deeply about what money means to them," Levin says. "The answer helps you sift through a lot of data to get down to the issue of fundamental needs or values."

◆ **Have you ever worked with a financial planner before?** "We want to know who it was and what the results were," Applegarth says. "That's enormously helpful." Likewise, if all the client's financial relationships have been negative, that's something you want to know, too. If the prospective client has moved from planner to planner looking for better performance, that should be a clue that you might never make him happy.

◆ **What do you want out of this relationship?**

◆ **Are you willing to commit to it for the long-term?**

SOME PROSPECTIVE CLIENTS DON'T make it past this first meeting. Most of the reasons planners reject clients have to do with expectations that are out of line. For example, successful planners will not take on a client who is focused totally on performance. "I turn away anyone who says: 'I'm getting a 24 percent return from such-and-such an advisor, can you beat that?'" says Ram Kolluri. Similarly, Mark Balasa turned down a small businessman who wanted help investing his pension plan after it became clear that "everyone who came across his path was an idiot," Balasa says. "It didn't take too long to deduce that we'd be the next idiots on his list, so we declined that one."

> *"I tell them I am not a*
> *performance pig and that*
> *I believe in managing all*
> *aspects of net worth."*
>
> — JUDY SHINE

Katharine McGee rejects clients who are not willing to go through the entire planning process. "I tell them I do comprehensive personal financial planning," McGee says. So the client might say, "I've just inherited $300,000, and I want to know what to do with it." McGee points out that the inheritance can't be dealt with in a vacuum. She asks them: Do you have estate planning documents in place? Are you participating in your employer's retirement plan? What is your marginal tax bracket? Chances are the client will say, "You're right. I need someone to tie this all together." If not, and they insist they want only investment advice, she refers them to someone who will do that.

"As a planner, it's just not personally satisfying to work like that," McGee says. "I am at a place in my practice where I can limit it to clients that are personally satisfying. I like the long-term relationship side of the planning process and that's what I prefer to do."

Although McGee says she is willing to gloss over money quirks in her clients to focus on the big picture, one man really put her to the test. This client, a man in his early eighties, had spent his life as a social worker and held very strong religious feelings about the morality of money. "He believes making money grow is evil," McGee says. "He told me early on that he would rather just put it in a jar and bury it in the back yard and let his kids dig it up when he died."

That would certainly be OK with McGee. But his wife, in her late seventies, "took a more practical approach," McGee says. "She taught school all her life and felt that she'd worked hard for her money and now wanted it to grow." And her husband is a man who believes that it is wrong to own two pair of shoes "because you can't wear them both at the same time."

McGee's solution? "I had to put the problem back in their laps," she says. "I couldn't solve it for them. I acknowledged their feelings. And I told them that between the two of them they had to come to terms with what it was they wanted from me." The husband backed off and said to the wife: "This is your money, and I'm not really concerned with the decisions you make." Now the wife comes to the meetings alone, and the husband is comfortable with the arrangement.

Mary Merrill prefers not to work with anyone with a "victim" sign around their neck. "I prefer to work with people like me who have a positive life philosophy," she says. "Likewise, I would prefer not to work with clinically depressed, recovering chemically dependent, or mentally unstable people; anyone who is hostile, secretive, paranoid, or close-minded; couples that are argumentative, bickering, and unpleasant; and people with extreme anxiety about money." Her ideal client is a corporate executive or physician with good self-esteem who is on the fast track and is looking for good people to help him achieve his goals.

Deena Katz looks for hidden agendas. Is the person in the room with her really the client? Or is the client someone else? "If they say: 'I have to go home and talk about this with my Uncle Fred because he's the money guru,' right away we realize that this is not the client, the client is going to be Uncle Fred," Katz says. That is going to make communication virtually impossible.

Greg Sullivan doesn't like to work with couples who are in conflict when they come in. For example, he worked through the interview process with a couple that bickered throughout. When he finished, he said: "Is there anything else I should know?" Well, the two replied, as a matter of fact, they *were* thinking of separating. Sullivan sent them elsewhere. "We have a good little practice here," Sullivan says. "These were just not the kind of people I would enjoy working with." Bill Howard doesn't want to deal with a "price shopper" or a "do-it-yourselfer." "These are people who aren't going to stay around for the long term," he says.

Every good planner rejects clients when they don't share ethical values. One example is tax evasion. So George Kinder had no trouble turning away a client who wanted him to invest $10 million in an offshore vehicle so he could avoid U.S. income tax. Peggy Ruhlin turned away a divorcing client who wanted to hide assets from a spouse.

Bert Whitehead will not work with any client who wants to conceal something—either from him or the government. Nor will he work with anyone he feels he cannot help. For example, he was visited by a couple in their mid forties who had retired with several million dollars. Both were heavy smokers and, Whitehead suspected, heavy drinkers. Their children were grown, and the couple said they didn't care about them. "There was really nothing I could do to improve the quality of their life," Whitehead says.

Eleanor Blayney's firm will not help a client with Medicaid planning. Not long ago, Blayney helped her own parents apply for Medicaid. "Having come out of that personal situation with my own parents, if a client comes to me to sequester assets, we would not do it," she says. "People argue that it is our ethical responsibility to our clients. But we don't do it." A 1996 change in the law that made it a criminal offense to apply for Medicaid within three years of transferring assets has reduced the options in this area.

Blayney also recently turned a client away at the second meeting because "he was very suspicious of all we said, and we were not getting off on a basis of mutual trust and respect," Blayney says. "I also think we would have a very hard time with couples who would not fully disclose material to each other." And the firm will not "push the limit in tax situations," she says. "It's a matter of deciding where you're comfortable."

When a prospective client comes in and the planner doesn't see it as a good fit, either because the prospect does not have adequate assets or because the chemistry is not good, many planners, like Bob Willard, will spend 30 to 60 minutes providing some advice pro bono.

Of course, Willard was not always so wise. Some years ago, when he was fairly new to the business of financial planning, he acquired some clients who were going to inherit $12 million. Both were professors. When they received their first stipend, for about half a million dollars, they told Willard they wanted to invest directly in businesses, like local retailers. "Because they had all those initials behind their names, I made the mistake of assuming they were sophisticated," Willard says, "and I helped them accomplish what they said they wanted to do."

The clients lost all their money, and their attorney gave Willard a call. "I was able to prove very clearly that I did exactly what they wanted me to do," Willard says. But he wasn't happy with the situation. "I reflected on it, and I thought: 'I am the professional. Why didn't I know that what they said wasn't what they meant?'"

That led him to start looking for correlations between personality and risk tolerance. Although he didn't find anything satisfying, he did learn that there is a difference in how clients and planners communicate.

"I realized I had simply failed to explain it on a level they understood," he says. Now he uses a subset of the Meyers-Briggs personality test to open discussions on risk-taking and goals. "It's a fascinating discussion because it really sets the stage for good communication," he says.

> *"If I feel really strongly that*
> *a client needs to do more*
> *than what they seem willing*
> *to do, I will really balk*
> *and say: 'It is not in your best*
> *interest to let this go.'"*
>
> —DIAHANN LASSUS

Other planners, like Harold Evensky, keep a stack of good books on personal finance and investing and offer one as a basic introduction. Most planners will refer the client to someone who might provide a better fit. For example, Greg Sullivan, who practices in the Washington, D.C., area, does not take government employees as clients. "It's just a different mind-set," he says. "They're not entrepreneurial types, generally. They're more safety conscious in their decision making, and generally they don't have the net worth and the income to really provide for a good long-term relationship for us." So Sullivan refers government workers to someone else. "We give them three names of planners in the area," Sullivan says. "Fortunately, Washington is an area that has a lot of planners. I feel that I can give them to a number of people around town that will actually do a better job for them than I would do."

Now That You're Engaged...

BUT IT IS THE CLIENTS WHO sign on that are most important. For these, there should be some sort of formal engagement process. Mary Merrill sends a questionnaire to those prospective clients who pass her phone screen and asks them to mail it back before the first meeting. At that meeting, they discuss goals and sign a contract that Merrill calls a service agreement, which outlines fees and procedures. The personalized engagement letter, which she sends immediately after that first meeting, reviews the discussion and the terms of the agreement *(see Chapter 11, "Sample Planner Documents," page 254)*. Planners who do not use a contract ask the client to initial and return a copy of the engagement letter.

Now the client is on board, and the planning process begins. That process can take several months. And most planners leave investments for last. Risk management, budgeting, cash flow, estate planning, college, retirement, and everything else come first. And before they get started on investments, good planners educate their clients about what kind of returns are reasonable to expect. Peggy Ruhlin requires her new clients to take a two-part course that she calls "Investments 101," taught by her or her partner, Jim Budros. Each session lasts two to three hours and gives clients the basics, to save her time later. "We don't really get to the investing for perhaps six months," Ruhlin says. It might take Bill Howard that long to get a plan in place, too. "We try to get people to see they need patience," he says.

Once the plan is in place, though, most clients need only tuneups. Many planners, like Ruhlin, meet with clients quarterly for 1½ to two hours for maintenance. Ruhlin has an agenda for each meeting. But often she sets it aside to talk about personal issues. "When you see each other that often, the personal stuff just comes out," she says. Greg Sullivan had a client come in to talk about investment performance, and the client said: "Do we really need to talk about this? There are some things I need to talk about." So Sullivan made his points, "and then we spent 80 percent of the time talking about his concerns," he says.

Sometimes clients aren't even interested in meeting frequently, once they feel comfortable that the plan is in place. Most planners are willing to compromise on the frequency. "We have some clients where we meet just three times a year or even twice a year," says David Homrich. "Things just kind of settle in, and you do what needs to be done."

Diahann Lassus has clients whom she can't get into the office for two years. "They're international travelers, or they're not around," Lassus says. "I have a client in Oklahoma that never leaves his lake." (Lassus is in New Jersey.) But she insists on frequent communication. "We try to meet once a year, but it doesn't always happen," she says. "So we communicate by e-mail or by fax or by telephone."

Even local clients are not always interested in sitting down to talk about money for two hours, four times a year. "One of my clients called my assistant and said: 'Would you tell Judy that I don't mind having lunch with her, but I really don't want to talk about money?'" says Judy Shine. "I thought it was pretty funny that she saw it as punitive to have to talk about money."

Planners might not demand to meet a specific number of times each year. But they do demand that clients address the agenda. The client must have an estate plan, a retirement plan, insurance, and all the basics in place. If a client doesn't get that done, it can backfire. It's the planner's job to make sure that doesn't happen.

"Whenever I've let a client get control of the process, and we haven't gotten the issues ironed out, then we've had to do firefighting down the road," says Diahann Lassus. "So if I feel really strongly that a client needs to do more than what they seem willing to do, I will really balk and say: 'It is not in your best interest to let this go. This is going to create problems for you down the road.'"

Each client also has an annual agenda. Most planners meet or talk with clients about it during the first quarter. "We meet with all our financial planning clients and retainer clients in the first quarter," says Bill Howard. "We want to get them in the habit of thinking: It's the first of the year. I've got to get things together for taxes, and I've got to see my financial planner." Shine asks clients at the beginning of the year: "'What is on your mind that has nothing to do with the stock market?' and we go through all the items like estate planning and teaching the kids how to manage money and sending them to college. So they give me their list, and I give them my list." Then Shine checks in with clients in July to make certain that those things are being taken care of.

Fee Breakouts

MOST PLANNERS ALSO TAKE CARE to make certain the client realizes what he is getting for his money. For instance, David Homrich charges fees based on a percentage of assets under management. "One of the things we are mindful of is that the client may forget all the financial planning work that we're doing," Homrich says. He responds to this by addressing it at the quarterly or semiannual meeting. "We make sure that the financial planning issues are always discussed, and we remind them of the work that we're doing," he says.

In addition, on the suggestion of one of his clients, Homrich makes a note on the invoice that the fee includes both investment management *and* financial planning services. "Then we give some examples of the things we've done for them in the financial planning area, right there on the invoice," he says. "We might say refinanced mortgage, updated estate plan, whatever the situation is, so that they're being reminded that they are paying for what we're doing, and it's not just for managing their investment capital."

> *"I think we would have a very hard time with couples who would not fully disclose material to each other."*
>
> —ELEANOR BLAYNEY

Diahann Lassus tracks how much time she and her staff spend with each client. "If there ever is an issue, we can literally print a report to show the client how many hours we've been spending on doing an investment review, looking at refinancing options, or evaluating an early-retirement package or a move to Florida," she says. For most clients, she puts the records in a file. "We try to focus them not on absolute dollars but on the value we're providing, and we really keep trying to come back to that," she says. But for the corporate clients, "the people who are really focused on hourly rates, for those guys I do summaries," Lassus says. "I can say we spent 25 hours during this time frame. That's important to know."

During the process, planners continually emphasize what they are accomplishing together—planner and client—and de-emphasize investment performance. "More and more, I think the value planners add is strategic as well as money management," says Judy Shine, who likes to track net worth. In January, she sends a one-page form to clients asking them to update numbers. "I try to stay off the whole stock-market issue," Shine says. "I tell them the market will take care of itself. I don't control it. I don't have a whole lot to do with it. We make our decisions, and then we pretty much let it rip."

Roy Diliberto decided the best way to find out what clients wanted was to ask them. In 1995, he set up a client advisory board to advise him on his practice.

Diliberto selected nine clients to serve staggered three-year terms on a board that would meet twice a year. "I tried to get a cross section of our clients," Diliberto says. "Some are retired professional people. Some are a little younger. We have people at various income levels." No one turned him down.

Before the first meeting, Diliberto sent out every report that the computer could produce, from performance to investment newsletters and other mailings. "We had them take a look at it, and they came in and told us what was important, and we changed our client reporting as a result of that," Diliberto says. He puts questions to the board about various aspects of his practice, such as whether clients like planning newsletters and what kind of performance reports and other mailings the clients want to see. The agenda for another meeting was what to include in an investment-policy statement.

At one meeting, he asked the clients why they hired him and why they keep him. Diliberto says he suspects that most clients initially hire him for investment return. But not one single client mentioned that. "I think they forgot why they hired us, but the reason they keep us is because of the relationship," he says.

His frustration is that potential clients do not understand that it is the relationship that they will value most highly. "How do you tell somebody that it is a relationship they really want, when they think what they want is for you to beat the S&P 500?"

Outplacing Clients

EVEN WITH THE BEST-LAID PLANS, there sometimes comes a time when a relationship is not working out. The two most common reasons are because the client has unrealistic performance expectations or because the client has become inactive and is no longer generating significant fees. In the first case, you should suggest a parting of the ways and offer the names of other planners. "Always give them other options," says Deena Katz. "You don't know who they know and who they're connected to, and you don't want to have things end badly."

If you have inactive clients or clients who don't generate enough compensation to make it worth your

Helping to Help Themselves

EACH PERSON CHOOSES his profession for a variety of complex reasons. Financial planners are certainly no exception. Understanding why you chose to be a planner can help you to be a better one. "The better you get to know yourself, the better you will be at your job," Dr. William R. Nixon Jr., a psychoanalyst from Birmingham, Michigan, told planners at the 1996 ICFP Retreat in Traverse City, Michigan.

Nixon suggested that developing a planner profile could also help distinguish the profession in the eyes of consumers, separating it from sales jobs like stock broker and insurance agent. Although planners see themselves as clearly distinct from salespeople, that perception is not yet universal. For example, Nixon said he talked with people on the golf course and in the elevators at the retreat to get a sense of how financial planners are perceived. "People don't differentiate between planners and salespeople," Nixon said. "They think you're all the same."

while, you might try restructuring your practice, the way Mary Merrill did in August of 1996. Merrill decided to move from hourly fees to retainers and to cut back from 100 to 80 clients. She set a minimum of $375 a quarter or $1,500 a year for a retainer. She sent letters to clients and offered those who were too small to meet her new minimums a free one-half-hour telephone consultation and a referral to another planner.

Katharine McGee has a process in place for determining when to drop a client. Once she puts a plan in place, McGee compares it to charting a course on a map. She's drawn the line with a felt-tip pen, and all the client needs to do is follow it. "They take it on their trip, and they guide themselves along the way," she says. At

Nixon provided his own quick planner psychological profile based on the research he'd done and the talks he'd had with planners at the retreat. "I think you're in this business because you have a hunger for intimacy," Nixon told the planners.

People who choose a helping profession like planning—or therapy—are trying to master something, he said. Many of them are struggling with traumatic things that happened in their own childhood. Perhaps your parents were not available to you in childhood, he suggested to the planners. "It might be the timing of sibs, the health of your mother, perhaps you moved 15 times before the age of 12," Nixon offered. A healthy way to deal with that trauma is to help others. "If there is a healthy ego, it will incorporate the trauma into change," Nixon explained. "Those of us in the helping professions are trying to help in a way that we were not helped ourselves."

But the same type of personality might suffer from rejection. "Self-esteem is *(continued on the next page)*

the end of the year, she sends an addendum that goes with her contract that must be signed and renewed every year. "At the end of the first year, if I haven't seen these folks, then I assume everything is going well, and I send the addendum out," she says. But at the end of two years, if the client has not come in to see her, sought her services, or updated the plan in some way, "I generally am not willing to renew that contract beyond that second year," she says. So she sends them a letter that says: "Obviously, you folks must be doing well. I haven't heard from you. You're in charge of your own affairs." She tells them they've graduated and does not offer to renew the contract, "because I'm not comfortable having someone consider me as their planner when I haven't done anything for two years," she says.

not the highest," Nixon said. That can end in a need to control; to feel uneasy when a piece of work doesn't get finished. "You all borrow from accountants an obsession with numbers," Nixon told the planners. "But you are more social." Many planners have a personality type that "wants to be helpful to the point of taking on jobs that are not best suited to you."

Given that you see something of yourself in this profile, what should you do? "What might you do to enhance the quality of your life as a professional?" Nixon asked. The danger of this planner personality is "that it has difficulties under extreme stress. A lot is expected of you." People come to you when they get lots of money or when someone dies. A typical planner personality might not be comfortable with the uncertainty inherent in that type of situation. The danger is the planner wants to solve the problem quickly: to get everything resolved, fixed. "It might be better, sometimes, to let it evolve," Nixon suggested. The planner personality also tends to become stressed in

And obviously, planners terminate clients who become abusive. Diahann Lassus terminated a client who was abusing her staff. "The only reason we figured out what was happening was because I answered the phone one day, which I never do, and the client started in on me, not realizing it was me," Lassus says. When she quizzed her staff, it turned out that this particular client always abused them on the phone. They never reported it, because "they just felt the client is always right, and they put up with it," Lassus says. She gave this client the names of other planners who are operating in smaller firms without staff people. "I felt uncomfortable doing it," she says. "But I personally never had any problems with this client and neither did my partner. So I'm hoping that will work out."

highly emotional situations "because you can't organize the data," he said. So planners often have trouble dealing with death, for example.

Planners also have a "proclivity toward grandiosity," Nixon said. They tend to be obsessive, compulsive, highly structured. That can make them convinced that their way is best and determined to get clients to agree with it. "A certain narcissism is healthy. But you sometimes would want your clients to have the same life as you. To have everyone live this life as we think they should is not healthy." Instead, planners should see their role as removing a client's problems with money. "I'm not in the business of making anybody be anything," Nixon said of his work as an analyst. "My job is to remove psychological obstacles." As a planner, you should think about whether there is room for someone to have totally different values from yours; to build a totally different life. "Can you live with it?" Nixon asked the planners. "Can you support it?"

MOVING INTO THE FUTURE

Think of financial planning as building a business to help people implement dreams. But don't neglect the nuts and bolts of building a solid practice and training advisors, either.

When he was 31, George Kinder fulfilled his dream of visiting Hawaii. To him, it was even more wonderful than he had imagined. He began planning to spend part of his life with the laid-back Hawaiians and their spectacular rain forests to balance out the buttoned-down life of the mind that he lived in Cambridge, Massachusetts. Kinder saved his money and stretched out his Hawaiian vacations until he was spending two months of each year on Maui. In 1991, when he was 43, Kinder took the plunge: He decided to spend May through October in Boston and November through April in Hawaii.

> *"The most successful people*
> *in the sales paradigm are*
> *the least qualified to do what*
> *needs to be done now."*
>
> — ROBERT VERES

As a financial planner, Kinder had some advantages in making his dream a reality. Much of his work is portable. When he mentioned his plan to his Hawaiian friends, they quickly offered to help him set up seminars and speeches to attract clients on Maui, as well as to refer new clients. Still, it required focus, the willingness to take risks, and hard work. "Much of my own personal financial planning was built around realizing my dream," says Kinder, who is now 48. For example, he saved a good deal of money. And then he used it to get his second practice going, rather than waiting for retirement.

Five years of living the life he chose for himself changed Kinder's approach to planning, too. Rather than harping on the virtues of saving, Kinder now sees his job as helping clients to implement their dreams. His question to new clients ("If you died tomorrow, what would you most regret not having done?") reflects that. Traditional planning places too much emphasis on retirement and the other dilemmas of planning, Kinder says. "The central question that people should ask about their lives is, 'What does freedom mean to me?'"

Indeed, most Americans still see financial planning as something punitive—like a crash diet—that denies them the pleasures of today so that they can set aside enough to eke out an existence in retirement. That perception contributes to the public image of financial planners as dreary taskmasters who will force them to forgo all the fun in life. And it is certainly one reason that many people put off going to a planner until their situation is desperate. All planners can learn something from Kinder: Financial planning should be about dreaming dreams and using your resources to realize them. To truly help a client enjoy a better-quality life, you must understand what his dreams are and help him achieve them.

Two Views

WHAT WILL FINANCIAL PLANNING look like in the 21st century? Will anyone need it? What types of planners will succeed? What changes will they make in their practices? We put these questions to a couple of people on the financial planning scene.

First is Robert N. Veres, an observer of the financial planning business for the past 15 years, first as editor of *Financial Planning* magazine and now as publisher of *Inside Information*, a newsletter that is read carefully by many of the industry's elite planners, and as editor-at-large for the *Dow Jones Investment Advisor*. Veres, who attends all the industry functions and spends much of every day talking with planners on the phone, never hesitates to call a spade a spade. Whether you agree with him or not, there's always something to chew on.

The second is Charles Haines, a University of Virginia MBA who worked with planners Lynn Hopewell and Don Rembert in Falls Church, Virginia, before setting up his own practice in Birmingham, Alabama, in 1986. In one sense, Veres and Haines are alpha and omega. Veres is the big-picture person, the dreamer. And, of course, he doesn't have his own practice, so he can afford to throw the net wide when he thinks about what planners should do. Haines is the pragmatist, a thinker who focuses on building a practice that will outlive him and that will be an asset he can sell. But they are both forward thinkers committed to excellence in planning, to its endurance, and to the changes that must be made to accomplish that.

I talked to Veres just after the ICFP Retreat in Traverse City, Michigan, just as the 1996 Summer Olympics were beginning in his hometown of Atlanta. The sea change in planning is behind us, Veres says. Planning has evolved from a sales business to a consulting business. "Ever since the Great Depression, the way people got financial advice was from a salesperson," Veres says. They bought insurance from an agent and stocks from a broker.

The laws that govern planners, such as they are, reflect that. For example, the Investment Advisers Act of 1940 was not really intended to regulate financial planners as we know them today. "The Advisers Act was created mainly for people running mutual funds," Veres says. "It had nothing to do with people advising you on your life." It remains a problem for planners, with regulators "trying to stretch a blanket over them that doesn't fit," Veres says.

The evolution has been painful. And there is still a long way to go, says Veres, who compares the discipline of planning to sex therapy in its early days: "It is such an intensely personal part of people's lives that it has a chance of becoming something more than it is now." But many of today's planners are not equipped to become what he calls "life advisors," like George Kinder. What used to make a stockbroker successful were sales skills. But what is needed now are people skills.

"The most successful people in the sales paradigm are the least qualified to do what needs to be done now," Veres says. "So they were the least qualified to make the jump." In contrast, those who didn't succeed in a sales environment may be the best financial planners. "The people who couldn't bear to touch all the money from the tax shelters are the ones who are doing so well now," Veres says. "They're the ones who are going to lead us out of this. The top producers are struggling."

A key reason for the change in planning is that consumers no longer need to be reminded to save money. "For years, people needed to be told to get in the game," Veres says. "Salespeople were appropriate." But today, most people realize that they must set money aside. "Telling them that is not a service anymore," Veres says. "When I see that there is $56 billion in the Magellan Fund, I can conclude that people do not need to be reminded to save money."

Those financial advisors who were trained in sales— most of them at the big wire houses like Merrill Lynch, Dean Witter, Smith Barney—are now struggling to retrain themselves in a field that has no training manuals.

At the top of the profession, some planners—about 10,000 of them, Veres estimates—have successfully moved from sales to consulting. He says about a third of the people he talks to at conferences are really financial planners, which he defines as someone who has a fiduciary relationship with a client and offers noninvestment services. But that's 10,000 more than there were a decade ago. "Ten years ago, when you went to industry meetings, everyone was talking about the hot tax shelter or the hot mutual fund," Veres says. But virtually no one is talking about sales today. "I ran into two people at a conference in Phoenix who were once sleazy tax-shelter salesmen," Veres says. "Now they're both fee-only planners, and they're both much more humble about what they do."

Yet sales left an unfortunate legacy. Because many of today's planners have a background in securities sales, they view the investment side of the practice as most important. "Those who made the transition from salesperson to consultant make the investment stuff a lot more complicated than it really is," Veres says. Some of them have even chosen to emphasize the investment side of their practice to the exclusion of comprehensive planning. "That's following the doctor model," Veres says. "Doctors have emphasized the technical stuff and de-emphasized services." But Veres doesn't think that model is the future. "That whole direction really concerns me," he says. "Investing is not rocket science. Once people find that out, they're not going to want to pay so much for it." Today, there are so few good people in the business that they can pick the clients they want, and they can choose how they want to practice. But that will not always be true. "There is this broad group of people that is catching up," Veres says. "I can tell by the dialogue at regional conferences that the profession is on the move again."

The profession is clearly moving to a fee-only business. But Veres sees asset-based fees as part of the painful transition planning is going through that puts the emphasis on investment management, chiefly because that's where everyone came from and where the advertising dollars are spent. "There isn't anybody spending millions of dollars in advertising to remind people to get a will," he says ruefully.

Meanwhile, the sales legacy has distorted fees, too. "The crude and foolish way to make the transition is to charge a lot more fees and to make it sound a lot more complicated," Veres says. That is evident in the current trend to charge fees based on assets under management and offering only investment services, he says. That means a client might be paying 1 percent simply for asset allocation, performance reports, and hand-holding. Veres thinks that's too much, particularly when other planners charge the same 1 percent and include comprehensive financial planning in that fee.

"Soon there will be a blockbuster consumer article

coming out that says: 'So and so is charging 1 percent for managing money, and someone else is charging 1 percent for everything,'" Veres says.

> *"If I had one piece of advice*
>
> *to give planners, it would be*
>
> *this: Think about your firm*
>
> *as a franchise business."*

— CHARLIE HAINES

One percent might not be too much. But to be fair, it must be allocated differently. "We're going to have to get down to 50 basis points for managing assets and 50 more on retainer for all other comprehensive financial planning to be in the right place," he says. Ten years from now, planners will look back on asset-based fees as a blip in the evolution of the profession. "When we come out the other side, we're going to realize that investing is a very small part of it."

Planners who have an eye on the future should be working to educate clients and build relationships. "We're living in an era of hideous financial illiteracy," Veres says. "That didn't matter in an age when everyone invested in a savings account." But all the rules have changed. Today, the social security system is on the verge of collapse. Americans must save for their own retirement with 401(k) plans. Cradle-to-grave employment is a distant memory. College inflation outpaces the overall cost of living. And there has been an explosion of financial instruments.

"You could argue that the financial markets are more dangerous today," Veres says. "They're not more volatile. But they are more dangerous." All of this means that Americans must have a lot more knowledge than they're being given in the education system. This is an important role for planners to play. "There's no mass communication initiative and no real incentive to do one," he says. "So it will have to be one client at a time."

The change of the past decade has been lightning-fast. But there is more ground to cover. In the next decade, planners will move decisively beyond investing, making that only a small piece of their practices, Veres predicts. "Stockbrokers will be where most financial planners are now. But they will be focusing almost entirely on the investment side," Veres says. The vanguard will be doing "real honest-to-goodness financial planning," Veres says, "which means dealing with all the issues surrounding money, including the emotional issues. Real financial planners will think of themselves as implementers of dreams, à la George Kinder, people who help clients realize their life goals.

"The next step is to become the financial sherpa, the general contractor of all financial affairs," Veres says. Key to that is educating the client and building a relationship; getting to know what the client wants, his innermost fears and dreams; and helping him accomplish what he sets out to do.

That's the soft side of planning. Our other guru, Charlie Haines, has spent a great deal of time thinking about how to build a planning practice that is a business. Regardless of their success as planners—and their income—most planners still have a job rather than a business, Haines says. That struck home for him when he joined NAPFA in 1995. Members of this group focus on competence. And on integrity. But few of them think about the longevity of their businesses, Haines says.

"They are a bunch of counseling-oriented people who are running boutique firms," Haines says. "You might be earning $80,000 a year, but you have to face up to the fact that what you have is just a job. Most planners don't have anything that anybody would buy."

Haines intends to build a business, rather than just a consulting practice, at his firm. And he thinks other successful planners should do the same thing. "If I had one piece of advice to give planners, it would be this: Think about your firm as a franchise business," he says. "If you wanted to franchise it, think about what the package would look like."

He was prompted to do that himself when he was asked by a major U.S. institution to consider starting some financial planning franchises in another part of the world. That isn't something that Haines, 41, feels able to do right now. "If I were older, if I didn't have children at home, and if we were handling our growth better here, I would just jump at the opportunity," he says. "But this isn't the time for me. There will be other times." Just to be safe, though, he's not talking about which institution did the asking or which part of the world is involved. Clearly, he wants to keep his options open.

Meanwhile, Haines is thinking about what his franchise package will look like and struggling with the issues of growing a business in largely uncharted territory. "We are going to be bigger than just a 15-person firm in Birmingham, Alabama," he says. "There is a great deal of opportunity in this field, and I'm just as excited as I can be. But we have got to be a business before we can show others that they can do it, too."

Haines is the first to admit that he has not solved all these problems in his own practice. But he is working on them. Here are some of the things he is struggling with and some of the solutions he has found.

Handling Growth

HAINES SAYS HE HAS BEEN influenced by the way Dallas planner Richie Lee structured his practice. Lee told a group of planners at the 1995 NAPFA Advanced Planners Conference in Tampa, Florida, that you can't sell your practice to an outside buyer if you're doing everything yourself. Delegate, he told them. Many top planners offer a handcrafted service. They do the marketing, sit down with every client and gather information, sit at the computer to develop the basic strategies, present the strategies to the client, and take client calls whenever they need additional help or advice. In order to grow your business beyond that, you need to add competent staff people.

> *"You could argue that the financial markets are more dangerous today. They're not more volatile. But they are more dangerous."*
>
> — ROBERT VERES

This has been a major problem area for Haines, who has been unable to add new planners quickly enough to take on all the clients who have come his way. "It is a real weakness in the system that we cannot hire or train or produce planners to fill the positions that we are in dire need of filling," says Haines, who was forced to turn away half the clients who inquired about services in 1995. "We had to turn away 10 or 15 doctors in December alone," he says. "We just couldn't handle it. You only can lose your reputation for providing good service once."

One of his strategies is to get the best and the brightest straight out of college. To do this, he set up a financial planning scholarship at the University of Alabama, which is the only accredited financial planning program in his state. The scholarship includes $2,000 a year and a paid internship at his financial planning firm. "The school recommends students for the award, and we interview them and then we jointly select the student who will receive the scholarship," he says. That means that he usually has a college intern available to help in his practice. And he also has a method to feed the pipeline with fresh talent.

He also hired two interns from U. of A.'s program, which has been operating for three years. And he has learned to leverage his own time by using an associate in client meetings to do some of the introductory work. "Jim Budros and Peggy Ruhlin really saved my practice, or my sanity, on this score," says Haines, referring to the planners in Columbus, Ohio, who are determined, like Haines, to build an enduring business.

His biggest frustration has been in recruiting top-level planners. After working with insurance and investment people, Haines has decided that the personal financial-planning division of the American Institute of Certified Public Accountants provides the best breeding ground for financial planners. "They tend to be more counseling-oriented," Haines says. He says he found insurance people to be too sales-oriented, without the analytical framework. "We're looking for analytically oriented people with personality. We don't want heavy personality, weak analytical," Haines says.

He recruited the head of personal financial planning from one of the Big Six accounting firms and was feeling really good about the prospects for growing his business when his new hire had a change of heart and decided to go into business for himself. So in late June, Haines sent out a letter to participants of the financial planning symposium of the AICPA in New Orleans, telling them about his practice and asking for recruits. "We're struggling with our growth, and we need help," he told the CPAs. "We're not looking for marketing help. We need doers." He is hoping to get some good candidates from that letter.

In his presentation to NAPFA members, Lee also suggested to planners that they begin to hire for niches. For example, you might hire somebody to concentrate on retirees, someone else for small-business owners, and someone who will deal with issues facing people with irreplaceable capital, like inheritors or divorcees. That, too, is on Haines' agenda, once he gets the basic people he needs in place.

Haines also raised his minimums—to a one-half-million-dollar portfolio or one-half million in income or some combination of the two. He has 85 to 90 portfolio-management clients with $125 million to $130 million under management. These clients must go through the financial planning process before they begin money management. There are another 50 to 100 financial planning clients who don't yet have enough money to begin portfolio management. "They met the income requirements but they didn't meet the assets," Haines says. "Either we are having them pay down debt, or they just don't have enough money." These clients come in every three years or so. Haines provides them with a debt-payoff plan and a three-year allocation. "They can't really hurt themselves or help themselves a lot with it," Haines says.

Time Management

TO BUILD A BUSINESS, YOU MUST know how time is spent by staff. Haines plans to use his new intern to look at how much time each person in the firm is spending on different issues; where the cases are profitable, where they are not; which fees were set correctly, which were not. He recommends a software package called "TimeSlips" (800-285-0999) for planners who want to get started on time management.

As a result of time analysis, Haines recently restructured the fees for the 401(k) portion of client assets because he found that his fees here were too low. Initially, he charged a one-time fee for providing asset allocation for a 401(k) plan. "We discovered through our time analysis that it actually took more time to handle the 401(k) assets in the asset-allocation process and in performance reporting," Haines says. "So here we were charging less for something that was actually more costly to deal with." Fees were revised so that the 401(k) plan assets are now part of the assets under management.

Staff and Structure

HAINES USES A ONE-PERSON "board of directors"—a retired financial planner named Abe Kaplan, who is now in his seventies—as a sounding board for his practice. Haines sends Kaplan reports, Kaplan analyzes them and makes suggestions. "I have to park my ego at the door when I meet with him once a month," Haines says. "He really hammers me. But his input has been really valuable."

One of the suggestions Kaplan made was to develop a procedures manual. "Abe said: 'Charles, you've got to have a training manual,'" Haines says. "A year went by, and he said: 'Charles, you've got to have a training manual.' Another year went by. We finally did it." Haines decided that when he hired the next new person, he would have that employee write down everything the staff told him to do. "You write our procedures manual," Haines told the new hire. "You're starting with a clean slate. You have no preconceived notions of what we do." This employee wrote down everything the firm does in dealing with clients from the time they walk in the door. Haines and others on the staff edited and revised it. Some of the things in the manual seemed obvious, Haines says. "But they weren't obvious to somebody coming in. So we need to have this out there." The manual has helped him build his practice, he says. "It's made it easier for me to delegate and let go, because we don't have to reinvent the wheel every time someone comes in the door."

Kaplan also suggested using an industrial psychologist on a consulting basis, which Haines has done. If a client has a problem, Haines reports it to the psychologist and the psychologist advises him on how to proceed. "She helps me figure out what they're going through and then coaches me on what to do," Haines says. "Only once have I asked her to sit in on a meeting with a client. But we tell people that we have retained somebody. It's another thing our firm does to help us better serve our clients."

The psychologist has also helped him see that portfolio management and financial planning are two different disciplines. Some time ago, Haines hired two employees who were both being trained in portfolio management and financial planning. "Finally one of them had the courage to say: 'Charlie, I just don't feel comfortable with the financial planning side.'" At about the same time, the other trainee said he didn't feel comfortable with portfolio management. So Haines decided each would specialize in one of the two areas.

"After that, we hired the industrial psychologist to test people to see what they're like and their interests and skills and so forth, and we discovered that we saw a trend," Haines says. For example, portfolio managers tend to be "thinkers" on the Meyers-Briggs evaluation, while financial planners tend to be "feelers." Now Haines is structuring his practice to accommodate that.

Haines also started doing client focus groups to find out what kinds of reports clients want. And he did his first staff retreat in the summer of 1996. "We've grown so fast, and we had some issues we needed to address," Haines says. For example, Haines prefers a horizontal management structure. But some of his staff members felt that they needed more direction. "So we're addressing that," he says. "We're just starting. We still need to do more."

As for his practice, Haines clearly expects it to be marketable. "This will probably be a private trust company that will have a market value," Haines says. "We may require some additional capital, which may require going either partially or totally public. But we are going to have an entity. It's not going to be over when the relationship with us is over."

CHAPTER

SAMPLE PLANNER DOCUMENTS

11

ALL PROFESSIONAL financial advisors need clear, concise documents to present to their clients. The two examples opening this chapter are reprinted courtesy of M.P. Merrill & Associates, Inc., in Madison, Wisconsin. Mary Merrill has provided both her Financial Planning Questionnaire and her Initial Retainer Agreement, which are given to new clients *(see page 229)*.

Following this, on page 282, is Harold Evensky's Annual Client Summary, reprinted from his book, "Wealth Management: The Financial Advisor's Guide to Investing and Managing Client Assets," published by Irwin Professional Publishing.

FINANCIAL PLANNING
QUESTIONNAIRE

OVERVIEW

To begin the process of personal financial planning, we will need you to complete this questionnaire. With the exception of the goal information, the information requested is quite self-explanatory. Most people have trouble completing the information on their goals. Don't be concerned if your goals and objectives seem rather general. Normally, as the financial planning process continues, your goals will begin to become more specific.

EXPENSE INFORMATION

If you wish us to perform a thorough cash flow analysis, we will need accurate information in this area. We realize it is time consuming to compile this information, as such you may wish to just make estimates for your various expenses.

LOAN INFORMATION

We will need very accurate information on any mortgages or installment debt you may have, since we prepare an amortization schedule for each debt. You may wish to bring along any loan summaries which were used to prepare your last year's income tax. If you have these, you will not need to complete the balance, payment, and interest information for the loans. Do, however, complete the description and creditor blanks.

ADDITIONAL INFORMATION

Other information which you should have available at our initial planning interview is as follows:

"INITIAL RETAINER AGREEMENT" AND "FINANCIAL PLANNING QUESTIONNAIRE"

1 Previous years' tax returns.
2 Statements or booklets relative to any group or employee benefits which you have.
3 Most recent annual statement for all life insurance policies.
4 Estate planning documents (Wills, etc.)
5 Information regarding any retirement plans.
6 Brokerage statements, mutual fund statements, and other information relative to any of your investments (e.g. Limited Partnership prospectus).
7 Disability income policies.
8 Salary, bonus, and other info. (Payroll stub, etc.)

CLIENT INFORMATION

	CLIENT	SPOUSE
NAME		
BIRTHPLACE		
BIRTHDATE	___/___/___	___/___/___
SOC. SEC. #	___-___-___	___-___-___
OCCUPATION		
EMPLOYER/ BUSINESS		
ADDRESS		
CITY/STATE/ZIP		
BUSINESS #	( ) ___-___	( ) ___-___
HOME ADDRESS		
CITY/STATE/ZIP		
HOME PHONE	( ) ___-___	( ) ___-___

CHILD/DEPENDENT	BIRTHDATE	BIRTHPLACE	S.S.#
	___/___/___		___-___-___
	___/___/___		___-___-___
	___/___/___		___-___-___

Educational Funding

CHILD'S NAME	CURRENT ASSETS	CURRENT COST/YR	# OF YEARS	% TO BE FUNDED

IMPORTANT INDIVIDUALS

	ACCOUNTANT	ATTORNEY
NAME		
FIRM		
ADDRESS		
PHONE	( ) -	( ) -

	INVESTMENT ADVISOR	INSURANCE ADVISOR
NAME		
FIRM		
ADDRESS		
PHONE	( ) -	( ) -

CHILDREN'S GUARDIAN

NAME

FIRM

ADDRESS

PHONE ( ) -

( ) -

( ) -

( ) -

	EXECUTOR OF HUSBAND'S WILL	EXECUTOR OF WIFE'S WILL
NAME		
FIRM		
ADDRESS		
PHONE	( ) -	( ) -

GOALS AND OBJECTIVES

Family

1 In the event of your death, what annual income would be needed for your family to maintain their standard of living? How have you arrived at this figure?

2 Have you thought about where your children may attend college? If so, what type of education would you like to be able to provide for them?

Financial

1 What are your near-term financial and investment objectives? Your long-term objectives?

2 How would you characterize your investment philosophy? (I.e. oriented primarily to: 1. long term capital appreciation; 2. balanced growth and income; 3. preservation of capital and buying power?) What are your secondary objectives?

3 Do you prefer making your own investment decisions, or do you prefer to have professional investment counsel?

4 Are you satisfied with the investment advice you've been receiving in recent years?

5 What have you done with your investment portfolio to minimize the tax bite?

6 Are you satisfied with the tax advice you are receiving?

Retirement

1 Can you look forward to retirement income from a pension plan or other source? Do you know at this time how much per year?

2 In order to gather all the necessary data on your company retirement and fringe benefits, we may need to contact the appropriate people in your company; who should we be contacting for this information?

3 Do you plan early retirement? At what age? At what level must you maintain your income?

Estate Planning

1 Have you a plan, including a will, designed to distribute your wealth the way you want it distributed after your death? When did you last revise this plan?

2 How satisfied are you with this plan? Does it meet both current and future objectives? If not, what areas of the plan would you like to see revised?

3 Do you hope to leave a substantial estate to your heirs? If so, explain.

4 To whom do you wish to leave your wealth: Your immediate family only? Your grandchildren? Other relatives and friends? Charitable bequests?

5 Do you foresee any special needs for any members of your family?

6 How important is it that your spouse have access and control of the funds left to him or her?

7 If there are any prospective family inheritances coming to you, give source and approximate amounts.

ASSET INFORMATION

Money Market Assets

Bank/Fund	Type of Account	Account Number	Account Balance

8 If you have previously been married, list resulting obligations.

Tax

1 Do you anticipate any unusual income for 1997, 1998, or 1999 which is not listed on your 1996 income tax return? If so, please list the nature and source of income.

2 If your deductions are likely to be substantially different from those shown on your 1994 tax return, please explain.

3 Do you see any radical fluctuation over the next three years, including salary bonuses? At what level do you anticipate that your salary will increase over the next three years?

4 Do you anticipate any radical change in your total net worth in the next three years? If so, what is the source?

Insurance

1 Have you made any contingency plans in the event that you become disabled? If so, what are they?

2 Do you carry any supplemental liability coverage? If so, how much? Please provide the details.

(Includes bank accounts, money market funds, CDs, etc.)

Interest Rate	Guarant.(Y/N)	Maturity(Mo./Yr)	Owner(H/W/J)	Pledged(Y/N)

ASSET INFORMATION

Securities

Description	Type*	# Shares	Face Amt.	Divid. Int. $/share	Purchase Price/Share

Tangible Personal Property

(Coins, stamps, bullion, etc.)

Description	Purchase Price	Purchase Date	Current Value	Owner (H/W/J)

Tax Advantaged Investments

Description	Amount Invested	Current Value	Owner (H/W/J)

* LEAVE THIS ENTRY FOR PLANNER
TAX CODE: R: ORDINARY N: TAX EXEMPT C: CAPITAL GAINS
TYPE: BD-BOND, GC-GROWTH COMMON, IC-INCOME COMMON, MO-MORTGAGE/DOT,
PS-PREFERRED STOCK, MF-MUTUAL FUND

(Stocks, bonds, mutual funds, deeds of trust, mortgages, etc.)

Purch. Date	Current Value/Share	Matur.(Mo./Yr)	Owner(H/W/J)	Pledged(Y/N)	Tax Code*

Other Assets

(Business, Pension Plans, etc.)

Description	Current Value	Owner (H/W/J)

Non-Investment Assets

Description	Current Value	Owner (H/W/J)
Personal property		
Automobiles		

LIABILITIES

Secured Loans

Description	Creditor	Current Balance	Interest Rate

Unsecured Loans and Revolving Credit

Description	Creditor	Current Balance	Interest Rate

Other Liabilities

Description	Amount	Owner (H/W/J)

Payment Amount	Payment Frequency	Maturity	Owner(H/W/J)	Pay on death H/W

Payment Amount	Payment Frequency	Maturity	Owner(H/W/J)	Pay on death H/W

(Not requiring installments)

Pay on death	
H	W

Estimated Sources of Income

	1997	1998	1999
CLIENT'S GROSS SALARY			
CLIENT'S BONUS			
SPOUSE'S GROSS SALARY			
SPOUSE'S BONUS			
COMMISSION			
INTEREST			
DIVIDENDS			
NET RENTS			
ROYALTIES			
BUSINESS PROFITS			
ANNUITIES			
TRUSTS			
ALIMONY			
CHILD SUPPORT			
OTHER INCOME			

Adjustments to Income

	1997	1998	1999
CLIENT'S DEFERRED RETIREMENT SAVINGS (401K, 403B, DEFERRED COMP., ETC.)			
SPOUSE'S DEFERRED RETIREMENT SAVINGS			
ALIMONY			
CHILD SUPPORT			
OTHER ADJUSTMENTS			

Real Estate Information

Asset Information

LOCATION

DESCRIPTION

CURRENT VALUE

OWNERSHIP (H/W/J)

Liability Information

LOAN DESCRIPTION

CREDITOR

AMORTIZATION DATA *

   DATE

   BALANCE **

   FINANCIAL STATEMENT AMT.

   PAYMENT (P + I) **

   PAYMENTS PER YEAR

   INTEREST RATE **

   MATURITY **

BALLOON PAYMENTS

1 DATE

   AMOUNT

2 DATE

   AMOUNT

3 DATE

   AMOUNT

4 DATE

   AMOUNT

CASH OUT DATE

FOR OFFICE USE:
FIRST REPORT YEAR

NUMBER OF REPORT YEARS

* IF YOU DON'T KNOW THE INFORMATION EXACTLY, YOU CAN ATTACH THE LAST ANNUAL LOAN SUMMARY PROVIDED BY YOUR BANK.
** NEED THREE OF THESE TO PREPARE AN AMORTIZATION SCHEDULE.

Living Expenses

	1997	1998	1999
Food			
GROCERIES	$	$	$
MEALS AWAY FROM HOME			
LUNCHES			
OTHER			
Housing			
MORTGAGE OR RENT			
PROPERTY TAXES			
HOME INSURANCE			
GAS & ELECTRICITY			
SEWER & WATER			
TELEPHONE			
CABLE TV			
MAINTENANCE & REPAIRS			
HOUSEHOLD SUPPLIES			
FURNISHINGS			
OTHER			
Wardrobe			
CLOTHING			
CLEANING & REPAIRS			
OTHER			
Transportation			
CAR PAYMENTS			
CAR INSURANCE			
GAS & OIL			
LICENSE			
MAINTENANCE & REPAIRS			
OTHER			
Personal Expense			
BEAUTY & BARBER			
DRUG SUNDRIES			
POCKET MONEY			

	1997	1998	1999
OTHER			
Education & Recreation			
TUITION, SCHOOL SUPPL.			
LESSONS & CLASSES			
SPORTING EVENTS, THEATRE, ETC.			
SUBSCRIPTIONS, BOOKS, TAPES, & CDS			
HOBBIES			
HEALTH CLUB			
VACATION			
COUNTRY CLUB			
OTHER			
Medical			
MEDICAL & DRUGS			
HEALTH INSURANCE			
DENTIST			
OTHER			
Life & Disability Insurance			
Other Expenses			
CONTRIBUTIONS			
CHILD CARE			
DUES, UNION, & CLUBS			
GIFTS			
BUSINESS EXPENSES			
PROFESSIONAL SERVICES			
OTHER			
TOTAL	$	$	$

CASUALTY INSURANCE SUMMARY

Homeowners

Description & Address of Property	Renewal Date	Policy Form	Company	Coverage Limits Liability

Vehicles

Auto	Renewal Date	Policy #	Company	Coverage Limits Personal Injury	Property Damage

Umbrella Liability

Insured	Renewal Date	Policy Number	Company

TOTAL PREMIUM

Dwelling	Personal Property	Loss of Use	Annual Premium	Deductible Amount	Comments

Medical Payments	Uninsured Motorist	Annual Premium	Deductible Amount	Comments

Policy Limits	Annual Premium	Deductible Amount	Comments

NOTES:

Life Insurance Summary

	Company/ Policy No.	Insured/ Owner	Policy Type	Face Amount	Paid-up Additions	Annual Premium
CLIENT						
TOTAL FOR CLIENT						
SPOUSE						
TOTAL FOR SPOUSE						
DEPENDENTS						
TOTAL FOR DEPENDENTS						
TOTAL FAMILY PREMIUM AND CASH VALUE						

Gross Cash Value	Loans	Net Death Benefit	Net Cash Value	Primary Conting. Beneficiary	Policy Value Date

HEALTH INSURANCE ANALYSIS

Medical Insurance

Insured	Company/ Policy No.	Policy Type	Policy Date	Basic Sickness & Accident Coverage		
				Max. Days	Surgical	Maternity

Income Continuation (Disability) Insurance

Insured	Company/ Policy No.	Policy Number	Policy Date	Monthly Benefit		Waiting Period	
				Acc.	Sick	Acc.	Sick

| Major Medical Coverage | | | | | | |
| Deductible | | | | | Premium | Annual |
Per Illness	Per Year	Ded. Amount	Co-Ins. %	Max. Coverage	Mode	Premium

| Duration of Benefits | | Your | Non | Guaranteed | Annual |
Acc.	Sick	Occupation	Cancellable	Renewable	Premium

Initial Retainer Agreement

THIS AGREEMENT is between M.P. Merrill & Associates, Inc. (the "Adviser") and

_____

with residence or place of business at _____

_____

_____ (the "Client").

1. SERVICES

_____ **A. Comprehensive Financial Advisory Services**
The Adviser will prepare a personalized, comprehensive analysis of the Client's entire financial situation and financial objectives. Adviser will provide written recommendations in regard to the Client's present financial position, tax and cash-flow management, investment management, retirement planning, insurance needs analysis, career or business planning, education planning, estate planning as well as other areas of financial concern as requested by Client. Adviser will work with the Client to coordinate the implementation of recommendations in the plan.

_____ **B. Investment Supervisory Services**
Once the initial plan has been developed, the Adviser will manage investments on a discretionary basis, based on Client's unique financial situation and written investment objectives.

To provide such management services, Client hereby appoints Adviser as attorney-in-fact with discretionary trading authority to manage Client's assets. The Adviser is granted authority to open securities accounts and give instructions to buy, sell, or transfer stocks, bonds, mutual funds, and other securities or financial instruments on Client's behalf. The Adviser will arrange for delivery and payment thereof, and act on behalf of Client in all matters incidental to handling Client's investment accounts. This authority does not grant Adviser authority to take custody or possession of Client funds or securities, except for payment of advisory fees.

The following procedures will generally be followed in managing individual investment portfolios:

1 Client and Adviser will agree upon written investment objectives individually tailored to the client's unique personal situation, liquidity and income needs, time horizon, attitude toward risk, and special investment concerns.

2 Client and Adviser will agree upon a long-term asset allocation which specifies the percentage of assets to be invested in stocks (stock funds), bonds (bond funds), money market funds, and other assets.

3 Adviser will recommend investments it believes are appropriate to Client.

4 Adviser will assist Client in opening accounts, filling out initial application and transfer forms, as well as remitting cash and securities.

5 Adviser may place transaction orders directly with investment companies (mutual funds) such as Vanguard and Fidelity, or discount brokers such as Charles Schwab. A small mutual fund transaction fee will be charged by Schwab that would not otherwise be charged if Client purchased no-load funds directly.

6 Adviser will generally use a "dollar cost averaging" approach when investing new funds, according to Client's objectives, and economic climate.

7 Client will receive prospectuses, confirmations, and monthly statements of all transactions from the broker processing transactions.

8 On a monthly basis, Adviser will generally review Client's account to be sure that it is consistent with Client's written investment objectives and asset allocation strategy.

9 On an annual basis, or more frequently if deemed necessary, Client and Adviser will meet to discuss Client's investment objectives, investment performance, asset allocation, and individual investments in the portfolio.

2. ADVISORY SERVICES TO OTHER CLIENTS

It is understood that the Adviser performs investment

advisory services for various clients. Client agrees that the Adviser may give advice and take action in the performance of Adviser's duties with respect to any of Adviser's other clients which may differ with respect to Adviser's own or Client's accounts. The Adviser shall not be held responsible for any loss incurred by reason of any act or omission of any broker of the Client's custodian.

3. RESPONSIBILITIES OF THE CLIENT

The Client agrees to provide information regarding financial circumstances, investments, income tax situation, estate plan, and other pertinent facts as requested by the Adviser in order to perform services under this Agreement. The Client also agrees to keep the Adviser informed of changes in the Client's financial circumstances and investment goals. The Client acknowledges that the Adviser cannot adequately provide the services requested by the Client unless the Client provides such information completely and candidly, and that the value of the Adviser's analyses and recommendations depends entirely upon the adequacy and accuracy of the information provided by the Client. The Client agrees to permit the Adviser to consult with and obtain information about the Client from the Client's accountant, attorney and other advisors (subject to the confidentiality agreement below), and to rely upon such information without verification.

4. CONFIDENTIALITY

All information and advice furnished by either party to the other, including their agents, attorneys and employees, shall be treated as confidential and not disclosed to third parties except as agreed upon in writing or required by law; provided however, that the Adviser is given absolute authority by Client to disclose, provide copies of, and communicate information obtained from the Client or developed by the Firm, to _____

_____

_____

5. BASIS OF ADVICE

The Client acknowledges that the Adviser obtains a wide variety of publicly available information from numerous sources, and that the Adviser has no sources, and does not claim to have sources, of insider or private information. The recommendations and advice developed by the Adviser are based upon the professional judgment of the Adviser and her employees. The Adviser does not guarantee the results of any recommendation or advice.

6. CLIENT AND ADVISER ACKNOWLEDGEMENTS

The Client and the Adviser acknowledge that the Adviser shall have no custody of the Client's funds or securities under this Agreement, and that the Adviser shall not have discretionary authority to direct the execution of investment transactions for or on behalf of the Client unless the Client has elected to use the Adviser's Investment Supervisory Service.

7. LEGAL AND ACCOUNTING SERVICES

It is understood and agreed that the Adviser and her employees are not qualified to and will not render any legal or accounting advice nor prepare any legal or accounting documents for use in connection with the Client's financial, investment, or estate plans. The Client is encouraged to obtain legal and accounting services from professional sources to implement the Adviser's recommendations. The Adviser will cooperate with any attorney, accountant, investment manager, or insurance professional chosen by the Client with regard to implementation of any recommendations.

8. FEES TO ADVISER

In consideration of the reports and services referred to in Section 1 (A, B, C) and selected by the Client, the Client will pay to the Adviser the applicable fee set forth in Schedule A.

9. TERMINATION

Either party may terminate this Agreement upon written notice to the other. If the Agreement is terminated prior to completion of advisory services, the Client agrees to pay the Adviser fees for all services rendered to the date of termination and the Adviser agrees to refund all unearned prepaid fees. Client may terminate this agreement without penalty within 5 business days of the date of this agreement.

10. MISCELLANEOUS

1 This agreement shall be applicable only to recommendations and advice prepared by the Adviser for the Client under this Agreement. It shall not relate to any recommendations or advice given by the Adviser or any person not specifically designated by the Adviser to perform such services under any other Agreements.

2 Neither party may assign, convey or otherwise transfer any of its rights, obligations or interests herein without the prior express written consent of the other party.

3 Subject to the provisions regarding assignment, this Agreement shall be binding on the heirs, executors, administrators, legal representatives, successors, and assigns of the respective parties.

4 This Agreement represents the complete Agreement of the parties with regard to the subject matter and supersedes any prior understanding or agreements, oral or written.

5 This Agreement may be amended or revised only by an instrument in writing signed by the Client and the Adviser.

6 The validity of this Agreement and of any of its terms or provisions, as well as the rights and duties of the parties hereunder, shall be governed by the laws of the State of Wisconsin, provided that nothing herein shall be construed in any manner inconsistent with the Investment Advisers Act of 1940 or any rule, regulation or order of the Securities and Exchange Commission promulgated thereunder.

7 Any controversy or claim arising out of or relating to this Agreement, or to construction or breach thereof, shall be settled by arbitration in accordance with the

Commercial Arbitration Rules of the American Arbitration Association. Such arbitration shall be before three arbitrators. Judgment on the award rendered by the arbitrators or majority of them, shall be final and may be entered in any court having jurisdiction thereof.

11. RECEIPT OF FORM ADV, PART II

By signing this Agreement, the Client acknowledges the receipt of Form ADV, Part II which discloses Adviser's services and fees, educational and business background, conflicts of interests, methods of analysis, and other information as required by the Investment Advisers Act of 1940.

Client Signatures:

By: _____

Date: _____

By: _____

Date: _____

M. P. Merrill & Associates, Inc.

By: _____

Date: _____

ANNUAL CLIENT
SUMMARY

Preface

MR. AND MRS. CLIENT, many of the illustrations in this plan involve the use of numbers because they are the most effective means of presenting a financial picture. These figures can lend an aura of false precision. Sets of numbers dealing with financial issues five years (and longer) down the road are not intended to be viewed as predictive but rather represent projections, based on a certain set of assumptions. Although real-life events can rarely be predicted with accuracy (e.g., your decision to retire at age 50; if and when you will sell your boat and second condo; your part-time work and the anticipated inheritance; the return on your land development; or the return on your currency hedge program), these projections are useful in comparing the likely results of different approaches and plans of action. If, upon reviewing this plan, you have any questions regarding the data or assumptions, please bring them to our attention.

Overview

BUILDING CAPITAL TO GENERATE (current and) future income is a primary objective of your investment policy. Our strategy for accomplishing this objective is

Policy material excerpted from pages 283–297 of Wealth Management: The Financial Advisor's Guide to Investing and Managing Client Assets, *by Harold Evensky.* © *Richard D. Irwin, a Times Mirror Higher Education Group, Inc. Company, 1997. Reprinted by permission of Irwin Professional Publishing.*

Sample Client ✦ January 1996

TYPE OF ASSETS	Personal & IRA Assets
CURRENT ASSETS	Approximately $1,275,000
INVESTMENT TIME HORIZON	Greater than 10 years
EXPECTED RETURN	4.5% over CPI
RISK TOLERANCE	Moderate to intermediate term
	Low to long-term
	Losses not to exceed 11% p/yr.
	With a 90% confidence level

ASSET ALLOCATION		
Cash equivalents	3%
U.S. fixed	37
Int'l fixed	5
U.S. large cap	24
U.S. small cap	11
International	15
Real Estate	5

ALLOCATION VARIANCE LIMIT/ BROAD CLASSES		
Quarterly	10
Yearly	5

REPRESENTATIVE EVALUATION BENCHMARKS

CASH EQUIVALENT	Donoghue Tax MMA
FIXED INCOME	Salomon 3 to 7yr Treas.
	Value Line Short Muni
	Lehman 5yr G.O.
	Lehman Aggregate
EQUITY	S&P 500
	Morningstar Growth & Inc.
	Morningstar Equity Inc.
	Morningstar Growth
	Morningstar Small Co.
	Morningstar Int'l
	EAFE

based on the concept of diversification, which we call asset allocation. It is a long-term strategy, designed to suit your individual aspirations and circumstances, which provides a durable framework within which to make specific investment decisions.

In designing your personal investment strategy we began by reviewing your objectives and constraints. We then developed recommendations appropriate for you.

INVESTMENT OBJECTIVES

◆ Before retirement, provide for supplemental income during your preretirement years in the amount of approximately $7,200 per year, after taxes.

◆ You wish to retire in three years and maintain your standard of living during your retirement. You estimate this to be $62,000 (after tax and in today's dollars) and $16,400 annually for 13 years for your mortgage payment. In addition, your families are long-lived and you believe that it is appropriate to plan for an income need for approximately 30 years.

◆ Factor in part-time income of $50,000 per year until Harold reaches 70.

◆ Provide for a wedding in two years. You estimate this to be approximately $30,000. You have reserved funds for this purpose.

◆ Provide for the purchase of a second home in Maine in approximately 2+ years. You estimate this goal to require $100,000 (in today's dollars).

◆ Provide for a portfolio that will be diversified and managed such that you can take an extended sailing trip through the Pacific and Australia without having to be concerned about your investments.

◆ Provide for gifting of approximately $30,000 per year for the balance of your life.

◆ Provide for at least half of the cost of a four-year college education at a major private university for your two grandchildren, ages 4 and 7. We estimate this to be approximately $12,000 per year, per child, in today's dollars.

◆ For the next three years, plan for the investing of future savings, particularly your $52,000 annual pension contributions.

◆ Preserve principal. Reasonable efforts should be made to preserve principal, but preservation of principal shall not be imposed on each individual investment.

◆ Reduce risk by diversifying markets, managers, and maturity dates.

INVESTMENT TIME HORIZON

◆ The investment guidelines are based upon an investment horizon of more than five years, so that interim fluctuations should be viewed with appropriate perspective. Similarly, your strategic asset allocation is based on this long-term perspective.

RISK TOLERANCE

◆ Building capital to generate future income is a primary objective of your investment policy. Our strategy for accomplishing this objective is based on the concept of diversification, which we call asset allocation. It is a long-term strategy, designed to suit your individual aspirations and circumstances, which provides a durable framework within which to make specific investment decisions. I know that you said you didn't want to hear, "You have to be patient, you're in it for the long haul." Unfortunately, it's true. Building your capital in order to protect your purchasing power from the erosion of inflation requires investments in the equity markets. Equity markets rise and fall with the business cycle. In simple terms, that means you need to have substantial investments in the stock market and those investments WILL lose money when the whole market goes down—and it WILL! The good news is that your current allocation to stock is more than adequate!

◆ In establishing your risk tolerance, we have considered your ability to withstand short- and intermediate-term volatility. Based on our discussions and your answers to our risk-tolerance questionnaire, we understand that you can accept a moderate volatility portfolio. However, based on your current portfolio and our capital needs analysis, we believe that you can comfortably accomplish your goals with a low-volatility portfolio and our recommendations are governed by your retirement goals. Note, however, that due to the significant nonrepositionable Life Annuity, our recommendation for your repositionable assets (referred to as the "managed portfolio") is growth oriented.

◆ Your strategic asset allocation is based on this long-term perspective. Short-term liquidity requirements are anticipated to be nonexistent, or at least should be covered by your earnings before retirement.

◆ Your personal income prior to retirement cannot be projected with any assurance. However, your expectations are that your new consulting venture will provide you with adequate income to cover your living expenses. In addition, between your personal cash reserves and your personal stock and bond holdings, you have adequate emergency reserves. Based on these assumptions, the policy for your 401K assets does not include any "emergency reserve."

◆ In establishing your risk tolerance, we have considered your ability to withstand short- and intermediate-term volatility. The results of our analysis of your risk-tolerance questionnaire and your current portfolio were somewhat contradictory. The answers to a number of our questions suggest that you have a very low tolerance for short-term volatility. Other answers, however, indicated a willingness to accept moderate volatility and your current portfolio is allocated almost 75 percent in the equity market. Finally, our analysis indicates that in order to approach your retirement goals, you must invest for growth. We have balanced these issues in our recommendations.

◆ In order to develop an investment policy for your nonsheltered investment assets, we have taken into consideration your IRA and pension accounts and the relative inflexibility of many of your investments.

◆ In establishing your risk tolerance, we have considered your ability to withstand short- and intermediate-term volatility. Based on our discussions and the composition of your current portfolio, we understand that you can accept, in the intermediate term, a moderate volatility portfolio. Although you indicated a strong preference for a low-volatility portfolio, your investments are currently almost 70 percent in stock. This includes your Exxon holdings for which you are taking significant, unrewarded, unsystematic risk. Your Exxon stock comprises over 40 percent of your current portfolio.

◆ Note that our recommendation is for a portfolio somewhat more volatile than that indicated by your answers to our risk-tolerance questionnaire. The decision to make this recommendation was influenced by our attempt to balance your clearly defined objective to maintain your current living standard, your acknowledged willingness to accept volatility in order not to lose your standard of living, a recognition that this investment portfolio does not include a significant investment in emergency reserves (i.e., the $50,000) and the fact that the recommendation will reduce your current exposure to the equity market and significantly reduce the unsystematic risk. If, in spite of these considerations, you are uncomfortable with our recommendations, we will revise the allocation and discuss with you the projected impact on your cash flow.

EXPECTED RETURN

◆ Our recommended portfolio allocation is for a moderate-growth portfolio of 45 percent fixed income and 55 percent equities. A reasonable expectation for the long-term rate of return of the recommended portfolio is 4.5 percent greater than the rate of inflation as measured by the Consumer Price Index (CPI). This expectation is based on the assumption that future real returns will approximate the historic, relative long-run rates of return experienced for each asset class in your Investment Policy. You realize that market performance varies and that a 4.5 percent rate of return may not be meaningful during some periods.

ASSET ALLOCATION

◆ We believe that your portfolio's risk and liquidity are, in large part, a function of asset-class mix. We have reviewed the long-term performance characteristics of various asset classes, focusing on balancing the risks and rewards of market behavior. The asset classes selected reflect your risk tolerance and the unique circumstances of your current investments. Six major asset classes were considered:

- ◆ **Cash equivalents**
- ◆ **Domestic equities**
- ◆ **Domestic bonds**
- ◆ **International equities**
- ◆ **International bonds**
- ◆ **Real estate**

The following securities and transactions were not considered: high-yield bonds, metals, natural resources, commodities or commodity contracts, short sales, or margin trades.

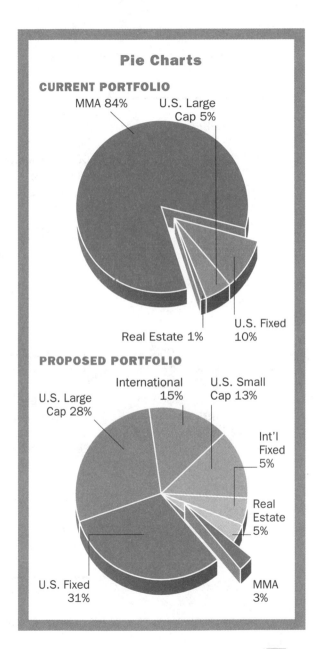

Investment Policy Allocation

Policy	Owner	Style	Description
MMA	Joint		MMA
	MRIRA		MMA
U.S. FIXED INCOME	Joint	SH Corp/Govt	T-Bills and Notes
	MRIRA		CD (6-Mo. Maturity)
	MSIRA	S/I Corp/Govt	"ABC" Short-Term Govt Fund
		SH Muni	
	Joint	S/I Muni	"DEF" Short/ Inter. Muni Fund
	Joint	Inter. Muni	"GHI" Intermediate Muni Fund
INT'L BO	MSIRA	International	New Int'l Bonds
			FIXED INCOME
U.S. LG CAP	Joint	Core	New Index Fund
	Joint	Tactical	New Tactical
	MS	Value	New L.C. Value
	Joint	Growth	"JKL" L.C. Growth Fun
	MS		IBM (recently inherite
	Joint		"MNO" L.C. Growth Fu
U.S. SM CAP	Joint	Value	New S.C. Value
	Joint	Growth	"PQR" S.C. Growth Fu
INT'L	Joint	Developed	New International
	Joint		"STU" Int'l Fund
	MRIRA	Emerging	New Emerging Mkt
REAL ESTATE	MSIRA		New REITs
			EQUITY
			TOTAL

Current		Policy		Proposed	
$30,000	3%	$30,000	3%	$30,000	3%
40,000	4			0	
60,000	6	60,000	6	60,000	6
30,000	3			30,000	3
170,000	17	70,000	7	70,000	7
		30,000	3	0	
110,000	11	110,000	11	110,000	11
150,000	15	100,000	10	100,000	10
		50,000	5	50,000	5
590,000	59.0	450,000	45.0	450,000	45.0
		50,000	5.0	50,000	5.0
		40,000	4.0	40,000	4.0
		90,000	9.0	90,000	9.0
130,000	13.0	60,000	6.0	60,000	6.0
90,000	9.0			0	
120,000	12.0			0	
0		70,000	7.0	70,000	7.0
30,000	3.0	40,000	4.0	40,000	4.0
		110,000	11.0	110,000	11.0
40,000	4.0			0	
		40,000	4.0	40,000	4.0
		50,000	5.0	50,000	5.0
410,000	41.0	550,000	55.0	550,000	55.0
$1 MM	100.0	$1 MM	100.0	$1 MM	100.0

YOUR PERSONAL INVESTMENT PORTFOLIO
Establishing the Fixed Income Category—
Proposed Allocation

Invest in the following fixed-income investments:

Money Market	$3,000
Short-Term Government/ Corporate Bonds	67,000
Short-Intermediate-Term Government/ Corporate Bonds	78,000
Short-Term Municipal Bonds	35,000
Short/Intermediate Municipal Bonds	122,000
Intermediate Municipal Bonds	111,000
International Bonds	56,000

Establishing the Equity Category—
Proposed Allocation

Invest in the following equity investments:

Large Capitalization U.S. Core	$55,000
Large-Cap U.S. Tactical	45,000
Large-Cap U.S. Value	100,000
Large-Cap U.S. Growth	67,000
Small-Cap U.S. Value	78,000
Small-Cap U.S. Growth	45,000
International Developed Equities	122,000
International Emerging Equities	44,000
Real Estate Index	56,000

YOUR RETIREMENT PORTFOLIO

YOUR TIAA IS INVESTED IN FIXED INCOME. We suggest that you move this to the CREF, which is invested in equities. The time horizon for these funds is at least 20 years. Your current IRA investments are also fixed income. We suggest that you place these funds in a U.S. Large-Cap Index fund (e.g., the Schwab 1000 or the Vanguard S&P 500). Again, the time horizon for these funds is at least 20 years.

MANAGER PORTFOLIO GUIDELINES
Domestic Equities:

◆ Equity holdings in any one company should not usually exceed more than 5 percent of the market value of the manager's portfolio. The industry sector weightings should not generally exceed 3 times that of the S&P 500.

◆ Equity managers shall have the discretion to invest a portion of the assets in cash reserves when they deem appropriate. However, the managers should, in accordance with AIMR standards, be evaluated against their peers on the performance of the total funds under their direct management.

◆ Equity mutual funds, if well diversified, should generally have moderate Betas and long-term positive Alphas, and less well-diversified funds should have favorable Sharpe ratios as compared to comparable style managers. Funds should have no loads and expense ratios less than 1.2 percent. The managers should have at least a five-year operating history and a consistent management record.

CAPITAL NEEDS ANALYSIS

IN CONJUNCTION WITH YOUR investment policy, you have asked us to address the issues of Capital Needs Planning to ensure that each income source is utilized in proper balance to create an adequate stream of income, including adjustments for inflation, throughout the balance of your life. Your investment policy is driven by this analysis and we incorporate projections based on our investment recommendations. However, the total return assumptions vary from the investment policy as noted in our assumptions for retirement.

Capital Needs Assumptions:

Inflation Projection	4.0%
Social Security Annual Increase	3.0
Taxes—Marginal	28

Capital Accumulation:

There are no projected savings.

Income Sources (in addition to capital):

Social Security while both boys are in school	$24,800
Social Security when William is 16 until he is 18	8,200
Pension from Exxon (no COLA)	4,056
Insurance Annuity (after tax)	14,800
Social Security after the "blackout" period	10,000

Income Needs:

Your expenses are classified, as necessary, into two categories:

◆ Inflatable-Basic—Nondiscretionary living expense

◆ Fixed Terminable—Home mortgage

CAPITAL NEEDS PLANNING CONCLUSIONS

THE CAPITAL NEEDS PROJECTIONS we've prepared are at best a very rough projection of the future. Your life expectancy and uncertainty regarding future income, growth of investments, and expenses are major question marks in the analytical process.

Based on the assumptions noted, we believe that you will fall short of your stated goals. However, you should keep in mind that these are long-term projections and incorporate many variables. We believe that the more short- and intermediate-term volatility you can tolerate, the more likely you are to improve your overall financial picture. We also note that returning to work and moving to a less expensive home will also add favorably to your financial future. We will discuss this with you, in detail, during our meeting.

FINANCIAL PLANNING OBSERVATIONS

Emergency Reserves As we have discussed, your emergency reserves are far in excess of any recommendation we might make for this purpose; however, we understand your desire to maintain a substantial cash reserve for your personal comfort and the investment recommendations reflect this.

As we have discussed, the recommended cash flow reserves are far in excess of any recommendation we might make solely for emergency reserves; however, we believe that maintaining a liquid cash reserve for your supplementary cash flow needs over the next few years is an effective way to manage your short-term needs.

Risk Management We suggest that you review your disability coverage, as well as property/casualty (renter's) insurance. You do not have an umbrella liability policy. You should discuss these issues with Mr. Brown, your insurance agent.

Based on our review, your health coverage with Exxon seems to be adequate. Your property and casualty umbrella is appropriate; however, the coverage on your antique furniture is inadequate. You should immediately have the furniture appraised and obtain a rider from your insurance company. It would be appropriate to take the opportunity to completely review your property and casualty coverage with your agent.

Given the substantial size of your estate, have your property and casualty insurance professionally reviewed, especially your liability coverage on your real estate, auto, and boat as well as your personal umbrella coverage.

We also believe that you should consider the purchase of individual long-term care policies, which meet the guidelines outlined in the attached.

You do not currently have adequate disability coverage. It is imperative that you obtain coverage. You should address this need as your first priority.

Tax Considerations The income from your pension, annuity, and the taxes generated by your significant investment portfolio are likely to keep you in the 28 percent marginal bracket. Our investment recommendations reflect this. If, after reviewing your taxes with your accountant, we find that your marginal bracket drops to 15 percent, we will work with you to adjust the investment portfolio accordingly.

As we have discussed, we recommend the sale of the

Exxon in spite of the significant capital gains that will be due upon sale. As we noted, the only ways to ultimately avoid the taxes are to die holding the stock, to wait until the market price drops to the basis price, or gift the stock to charity. The first two choices are clearly unacceptable, and, with the exception of minor gifting to Big Brothers/Big Sisters, charitable strategies are not a viable alternative. By delaying the sale, taxes are not avoided but merely deferred. The savings are the present value of the possible earnings on the deferred taxes. This is not an adequate reward for accepting the unsystematic risk associated with holding one unmanaged stock position.

Estate Planning Your current estate planning documents incorporate guardianship and trusts for your sons. We suggest that you also consider the possibility of establishing a living (revocable) trust. Although a living trust is frequently recommended for the purpose of probate avoidance, we do not consider that, in and of itself, an adequate justification. The primary reason we recommend consideration of such a trust is to pre-arrange for the management of your affairs in the event of your incapacity. We also strongly recommend that you consider the preparation of a durable power of attorney, a health care power, and a "living" will.

We will be happy to discuss these issues with your other advisors (with your permission) and/or refer you to knowledgeable professionals should you request any assistance in these matters.

RESOURCES
& ADDITIONAL READING

FINANCIAL PLANNERS MUST DO a lot of reading to keep up with both their profession and all the issues faced by their clients. The publications they rely on are discussed in detail in Chapter 1, "Education and Training." This section is aimed at those trying to get a toehold in planning and the issues involved.

When I told people I know in the financial planning business that I was working on a guidebook for planners, the first name on everyone's lips was that of Katherine Vessenes. Vessenes, a lawyer and certified financial planner, worked for a time with American Express Financial Services. She speaks frequently on financial planning issues, most especially on compliance. Her guidebook, *Protecting Your Practice,* which covers compliance basics, was published in 1997 by Bloomberg Press in cooperation with the International Association for Financial Planning, now the Financial Planning Association.

When regulation of financial planners is split between the Securities and Exchange Commission (for planners who manage more than $25 million) and the states, beginning in April 1997, more advisors will be audited. The SEC says it will audit the advisors it regulates at least every five years.

There are a number of resources available to help with compliance issues. In fall 1996, Jeffrey B. Kelvin, president and chief executive officer of Financial Planners Assistance Corp., a Conshohocken, Pennsylvania-based company that provides legal counsel for advisors, launched the RIA's Compliance Survival Toolkit software and worksheets to help with tasks ranging from registering to preparing for an audit.

"The Money Manager's Compliance Guide," published by Thompson Publishing Group Inc. in Washington, D.C., outlines procedures and regulations and includes monthly updates.

National Regulatory Services in Lakeville, Connecticut, offers ComplyNet, an online service with daily updates and information on filings and proposals from the Securities and Exchange Commission, the National Association of Securities Dealers, and various states. The service is available on the World Wide Web. Charles Schwab Corp. offers ComplyNet to advisors, and Fidelity Investment Advisor Group offers the information in a monthly newsletter.

There are a number of publications that are read by planners as well as knowledgeable lay people. I won't mention the obvious, like *Forbes* and *The Wall Street Journal.* But a good, but less obvious, choice is *Institutional Investor* magazine. This monthly is written for investment and finance professionals and often includes cutting-edge articles on pensions and money management, for example.

While I was working on this book, I read the industry publications like the *Investment Advisor* (732-389-8700) as well as *Financial Planning* magazine and *Registered Representative* (800-811-3255). These three publications address many of the regulatory issues that face financial planners, as well as marketing and servicing clients.

I write for *Bloomberg Wealth Manager* (800-681-7727), which also has a useful Web site, http://wealth.bloomberg.com.

Robert N. Veres, former editor of *Financial Planning* magazine and a familiar figure on the planning lecture circuit, publishes *Inside Information,* a newsletter, ten times a year. This is a must-read for planners. Admitting you don't subscribe relegates you to the ranks of the second tier. Don Phillips, president of Morningstar, claims that Veres' newsletter is one of two things that he reads immediately when he receives it. In his annual, *Meetings Year in Review,* Veres provides an overview of each of the major industry meetings, subjects covered, what was worth hearing, and what you can learn from it. If you can't attend the meetings, read this. If you attended but didn't make it to all the sessions, read this.

The other publication that Phillips reads immediately when it hits his desk is *Outstanding Investor Digest,* published by Henry Emerson. The *Digest* goes for $495 for ten issues, although you can get it for $295 if you agree to an automatic credit-card payment (212-925-3885).

For investment information, everyone uses *Morningstar Mutual Funds.* Many planners also use Value Line. Most also use the Ibbotson database.

Planners must also keep abreast of arcane regulatory changes in areas like taxes and pensions. Laura Tarbox, a CFP in Newport Beach, California, subscribes to *Taxline,* a monthly letter published by the National Underwriter ($48 a year), because it covers the really obscure stuff in the areas she most needs information: life insurance, pensions, retirement, investments. She also receives the annual "TaxFacts I," which covers insurance and retirement plans, and "TaxFacts II," which covers rulings involving stocks, bonds, and mutual funds. The two books cost $37 (800-543-0874).

THERE IS LOTS OF INFORMATION for planners on the Internet. Here are some of the places to get started:

◆ **American Stock Exchange**: http://www.amex.com
◆ **Bank Rate Monitor Infobank**: http://www.bank rate.com
◆ *Barron's*: http://www.barrons.com
◆ *Bloomberg Personal Finance*: http://www.bloom berg.com
◆ **CNNfn**: http://www.cnnfn.com
◆ **Ernst & Young**: http://www.ey.com/us/tax
◆ **Financenter**: http://www.financenter.com
◆ **The Financial Data Finder, Ohio State University**: http://www.cob.ohio-state.edu:80/dept/fin/overview .htm
◆ **Financial Planning Association**: http://www.fpanet .org
◆ *Financial Planning* **Online**: http://www.fponline.com
◆ *Forbes*: http://www.forbes.com
◆ **Ibbotson Associates**: http://www.ibbotson.com/
◆ *Investors Business Daily*: http://www.investors.com
◆ **Nasdaq**: http://www.nasdaq.com
◆ **National Association of Securities Dealers Regulation:** http://www.nasdr.com
◆ **NetWorth**: http://www.Quicken.com.investments
◆ **New York Stock Exchange**: http://www.nyse.com
◆ *The New York Times*: http://www.nytimes.com
◆ **Securities and Exchange Commission**: http:// www.sec.gov
◆ *The Wall Street Journal*: http://www.wsj.com
◆ **William Sharpe**: http://www.stanford.edu/~wfsharpe/
◆ *Worth*: http://www.worth.com

Books Mentioned

Applegarth, Ginger. "The Money Diet: Reaping the Rewards of Financial Fitness" [Penguin USA, 1996; $12.95]

Baldwin, Ben G. "The New Life Insurance Investment Advisor" [Probus Publishing Co., 1994; $24.95]

Bateson, Mary Catherine. "Composing a Life" [Plume, 1990; $11.95]

Black, Henry C. (et al). "Black's Law Dictionary" [6th edition, West Pub., 1993; $29.50]

Covey, Stephen R. "The 7 Habits of Highly Effective People" [Fireside/Simon & Schuster Trade, 1990; $14.00]

DePree, Max. "Leadership Is an Art" [Dell Trade Paperbacks, 1990; $12.95]

Drucker, Peter F. "The New Realities" [Harper Business, 1994; $13.00]

Ellis, Charles. "Investment Policy, Reinhardt Werba Bowen Advisory Services Special Edition: How to Win the Losers Game" [Irwin Professional Publishing, 1993; $16.45]

Evensky, Harold R. "Wealth Management: The Financial Advisor's Guide to Investing & Managing Client Assets" [Irwin Professional Publishing, 1996; $50.00]

Gibson, Roger C. "Asset Allocation: Balancing Financial Risk" [Irwin Professional Publishing, 1996; $50.00]

Goldberg, Seymour, J.K. Lasser. "J.K. Lasser's How to Pay Less Tax on Your Retirement Savings" [MacMillan General Reference, 1996; $15.95]

―――. "Professional's Guide to the IRA Distribution Rules" [2nd rev. ed., Foundation for Accounting Education, (212) 719-8300, 1993; $37.50]

Gourgues, Harold W. and Homrich, David E. "Total Financial Planning: A Guide for Advisors & Serious Investors" [NY Institute of Finance, 1988; $64.95]

Grudin, Robert. "The Grace of Great Things: On the Nature of Creativity" [Ticknor & Fields, 1991; $12.95]

Gurney, Kathleen. "Your Money Personality: What It Is and How You Can Profit From It" [Doubleday, 1988]

Hausner, Lee. "Children of Paradise: Successful Parenting for Prosperous Families" [J.P. Tarcher, 1990; $18.95]

Kennedy, Paul M. "The Rise & Fall of the Great Powers: Economic Change & Military Conflict from 1500 to 2000" [Vintage Books, 1989; $16.00]

Landsburg, Steven E. "The Armchair Economist: Economics & Everyday Life" [Free Press, 1995; $12.00]

Levin, Ross. "Wealth Management Index: The Financial Advisor's System for Assessing & Managing Your Client's Plans & Goals" [Irwin Professional Publishing, 1996; $50.00]

Mackay, Charles. "Extraordinary Popular Delusions & the Madness of Crowds," with foreword by

Andrew Tobias. [Crown Publishing/Random, 1995; $14.00]

Mellan, Olivia. "Money Harmony: Resolving Money Conflicts in Your Life & Relationships" [Walker & Co., 1995; $9.95]

Murray, Nick. "Serious Money: The Art of Marketing Mutual Funds" [R. A. Stanger, 1991; $34.50]

————. "Gathering Assets: The Best of Nick Murray" [R.A. Stanger, 1995; $24.50]

"Robin Hood was Right: A Guide to Giving Your Money for Social Change." [Bookpeople, 1978; not currently available]

Rowland, Mary. "A Commonsense Guide to Mutual Funds" [Bloomberg Press, 1996; $19.95]

Schwartz, Peter. "The Art of the Long View: Planning for the Future in an Uncertain World" [Doubleday, 1996; $15.00]

Train, John. "The New Money Masters" [Harper Business, 1994; $13.00]

Trone, Donald; with William R. Allbright, Philip R. Taylor. "The Management of Investment Decisions" [Irwin Professional Publishing, 1995; $65.00]

Vessenes, Katherine. "The Compliance & Liability Handbook for Financial Planners and Financial Service Professionals" [International Association for Financial Planning, 1992]

About Bloomberg

Bloomberg L.P., founded in 1981, is a global information services, news, and media company. Headquartered in New York, the company has nine sales offices, two data centers, and 85 news bureaus worldwide.

Bloomberg, serving customers in 126 countries around the world, holds a unique position within the financial services industry by providing an unparalleled range of features in a single package known as the BLOOMBERG PROFESSIONAL™ service. By addressing the demand for investment performance and efficiency through an exceptional combination of information, analytic, electronic trading, and Straight Through Processing tools, Bloomberg has built a worldwide customer base of corporations, issuers, financial intermediaries, and institutional investors.

BLOOMBERG NEWSˢᴹ, founded in 1990, provides stories and columns on business, general news, politics, and sports to leading newspapers and magazines throughout the world. BLOOMBERG TELEVISION®, a 24-hour business and financial news network, is produced and distributed globally in seven different languages. BLOOMBERG RADIO™ is an international radio network anchored by flagship station BLOOMBERG® WBBR 1130AM in New York.

In addition to the BLOOMBERG PRESS® line of books, Bloomberg publishes *BLOOMBERG® MARKETS, BLOOMBERG PERSONAL FINANCE™*, and *BLOOMBERG® WEALTH MANAGER.* To learn more about Bloomberg, call a sales representative at:

Frankfurt:	49-69-92041-200	São Paulo:	5511-3048-4500
Hong Kong:	85-2-2977-6600	Singapore:	65-212-1200
London:	44-20-7330-7500	Sydney:	61-2-9777-8601
New York:	1-212-318-2200	Tokyo:	81-3-3201-8950
San Francisco:	1-415-912-2980		

About the Author

Mary Rowland is a distinguished columnist and author specializing in financial planning and practice management issues. She was the personal finance columnist for the Sunday *New York Times* from 1989 to 1995. She writes regular columns for Microsoft Investor at www.moneycentral.com, for *Bloomberg Wealth Manager* magazine, and for that magazine's Web site at http://wealth.bloomberg.com. Her work has appeared in *Fortune, Business Week, Worth, Investment Advisor, Institutional Investor, USA Today, Modern Maturity,* and many other publications. For twenty-five years she has looked at financial planning from both sides, interviewing financial advisors and portfolio managers for professional journals and writing for consumers on such topics as selecting a financial planner.

She is the author of three other books: *The Fidelity Guide to Mutual Funds, A Commonsense Guide to Your 401(k),* and *The New Commonsense Guide to Mutual Funds.* Ms. Rowland appears frequently on television and radio and speaks regularly to business and consumer groups and to financial advisors.